What people are saying about
ACADIAN REDEMPTION:
From *Beausoleil* Broussard to
the Queen's Royal Proclamation:

"...a fascinating and most unusual book... [readers] will find the account refreshing as few histories recount the struggle against the British expulsion, and almost none follow the story of a single individual. In at least two senses, Warren Perrin has changed history – into His Story."

-Robert Bridges, *Cajun Times*

"This really is a nice little book and would make an excellent stocking stuffer for Broussard descendants... definitely an interesting read."

-Damon Veach, *The Advocate Magazine*

"While preparing a presentation on Joseph *dit Beausoleil* Broussard... Perrin realized that no one had written a book on the life of this heroic Acadian. Perrin has corrected this oversight by compiling an interesting book on an Acadian freedom fighter who resisted British aggression and ultimately led his people from Acadia to a new life in Southwest Louisiana."

 la Louisiane

D1501701

ACADIAN REDEMPTION:

*From **Beausoleil** Broussard*
to the Queen's Royal Proclamation

WARREN A. PERRIN

First Trade Edition
May, 2005

Warren A. Perrin

Andrepont Publishing, L.L.C.
326 Cedar Grove Drive
Opelousas, Louisiana 70570
(800) 738-2500

———————————

ISBN 0-9768927-0-7 (previously ISBN 0-9704073-1-9)

Printed in the United States of America

ACADIAN REDEMPTION

TABLE OF CONTENTS

Maps, Documents and Illustrations

ACADIAN REDEMPTION:

From *Beausoleil* Broussard to the Queen's Royal Proclamation

If we stand tall, it is because we stand on the shoulders of many ancestors.

- Yoruba proverb

ACKNOWLEDGEMENTS

The genesis for this book was the first *Congrès Mondial Acadien 1994*. However, my decision to go forward came in 2003. I was invited by Sheila Broussard of Halifax, Nova Scotia, to make a joint presentation on August 11, 2004, during the *Congrès Mondial Acadian 2004* with Alfred Silver, renowned Nova Scotian writer, on Joseph *dit Beausoleil* Broussard at the Broussard Family Reunion in the Village of Pomquet, Antigonish County, Nova Scotia. As I worked to prepare a draft of my talk, I realized that no one had written a book on *Beausoleil's* life, and that there were many contradictory facts found in various articles written about him. After the Queen's Royal Proclamation was signed on December 9, 2003, I decided this book could be a way of combining Acadian history with this contemporary event.

As with most books, this one required a cumulative effort of many individuals and groups who responded to my frequent pleas for assistance, including Chris Segura, Ryan Brasseaux, Dr. John Mack Faragher, Donald Arceneaux, George Bentley, Shane K. Broussard, Jason Theriot, Earlene Broussard, Maurice Basque, Zachary Richard, Louise McKinney, James Louviere, Brenda Comeaux Trahan, Dr. Carl A. Brasseaux, Sam Broussard, Don Louis Broussard, and Meera Sundram. My deepest thanks go to each of you.

This project was funded in part by the Acadian Heritage and Cultural Foundation, a non-profit corporation that operates the Acadian Museum of Erath. My heartfelt appreciation goes to all members and board of directors, cultural representatives and volunteers, especially Director Kermit Bouillion, Ron Miguez, head of museum operations, Clement Bourgeois, Jr., Simon Broussard, J. N. Broussard, Terry Perrin, and Russell Gary.

The museum patrons who have served on the board are J. Weldon Granger, Esquire; Dr. Carl Brasseaux, Director of Center for Louisiana Studies, University of Louisiana at Lafayette; Dr. James H. Dormon, former Head, History Department, University of Louisiana at Lafayette (retired); U. S. Senator John Breaux; Paul Hardy, Lt. Governor of Louisiana, (retired); Michel Doucet, Dean of Law School, *Université de Moncton*; Fernard deVarennes, Murdoch University, Perth, Australia; Senator Gerald Comeau, Senate of Canada; Honorable Melinda Schwegmann, former Lt. Gov. of Louisiana; Richard Dubois, Gulf Coast

Bank; Claudette Lacour, Erath 4th of July Association; U. S. Senator George Mitchell, Maine (retired); Jimmy C. Newman; Rev. Patrick Primeaux, Ph.D., St. John's University; Leon David Ortemond; George Dupuis, Jr., Mayor of Erath; Judge Charles L. Porter, 16th Judicial District Court; D. L. Menard; Earl Broussard and Stephen Granger.

Thanks to the museum's Deputy Patrons: Dr. Mathé Allain, University of Louisiana at Lafayette; Dr. Barry Ancelet, former head of Department of Modern Languages, University of Louisiana at Lafayette; Trent Angers, Editor, *Acadiana Profile*; Senator Allen Bares (retired); Alton Broussard, II; Father Wayne Duet, Our Lady of Lourdes Catholic Church; Dr. Phillip F. Dur, University of Louisiana at Lafayette, (retired); Judge J. Burton Foret, Court of Appeals (retired); Russell R. Gaspard, Vermilion Parish Clerk of Court (retired); Raymond LaLonde, Louisiana House of Representatives (retired); Belva LeBlanc; Cecil Picard, Louisiana Superintendent of Education; Father Joseph Henry Stemmann; Una Broussard Evans, Vermilion Historical Society; Pete Bergeron, KRVS Radio, University of Louisiana at Lafayette; Philippe Gustin, *Le Centre International de Lafayette*; Daniel Broussard, Vermilion Parish Assessor, (retired); Yvon Fontaine, former Dean of the University of Moncton, Canada, (retired); Gerard Johnson; A. J. LeBlanc, Lafayette; Robert Vincent; Carey LeBlanc; Earlene Broussard; Mark Poché, President of the Vermilion Parish Policy Jury; Allen Simon; Lynn Breaux; Gladys Romero; Dr. Shane K. Bernard; Marla LeBlanc Doolin; and Whitney Lynn Broussard, Chairman, Historical Collections.

My sincere thanks to the Executive Committee: Tom Angers, Esquire; Ned Arceneaux, Professor Christopher Blakesley, Louisiana State University Law Center; Leonce and Emilia Blanchard, Canada; Professor Leon Theriault, *Université de Moncton*; Sam Theriot, former Vermilion Parish Clerk of Court; Jim Bradshaw; Charles E. Broussard; John C. Broussard, Acadian activist; Professor Jacques Henry, University of Louisiana at Lafayette; Thomas E. Guilbeau, Esquire; Marc W. Judice, Esquire; Ron Guidry; Dr. Gary Marotta, State University of New York at Buffalo; Ray Mouton, Jr., Esquire; John L. Olivier, Esquire; Glen Pitre; Philip Parent, Esquire, Maine; Virgil C. Reid; Christopher Rose; Gerard Sellers; Michel Tauriac; Mike Thibodeaux; Dudley J. Young and Tommy LeBlanc.

The following were very helpful, including Gale Luquette, Shane Landry, Judge Durwood Conque, Judge Herman Clause, Judge Rick

Michot, Judge Byron Hebert and George Sfeir.

The following, now deceased, were very supportive during their lifetimes: Judge Cleveland J. Frugé; Howard E. Crosby, Canadian House of Commons; Marcus Broussard III; Frederick M. delaHoussaye; Wilfred Doucette; Judge Bennett Gautreaux; Monsignor Jules O. Daigle, M.A., S.T.L.; René Babineau, *Club International des Acadiens*; Richard Baudoin; Lou Ella Menard; Presley LeBlanc; Evelyn G. Boudreaux; Brent Broussard; Relie LeBlanc, III; Cleve Thibodeaux and J. Maxie Broussard.

Special thanks to Darylin Barousse and Sharon Newman, who typed the manuscript, and Terry Perrin, Don Louis Broussard, Mitch Conover, James Louviere, Chére Coen, Earlene Broussard, Madeline Bourque, Allison Dickerson, Billie Wayne Broussard, Brenda Trahan, Charles Broussard, George Bently, Donald Arceneaux, Daniel Paul (Mi'Kmaq historian and human rights activist), Maxine Duhon, Michel Roux and Jason Theriot, who proof-read this work for me. I thank my current law partners Donald D. Landry, Gerald C. deLaunay, Scott A. Dartez and Jean Ouellet.

Merci beaucoup to Dr. David Cheramie, Executive Director and the Board of Directors of the Council for the Development of French in Louisiana (CODOFIL), staff members Elaine Clément and Jennifer Miguez, and my mentor Judge Allen M. Babineaux, who died August 23, 2004. Thanks to John Hernandez, Jr., John Hernandez, III, David Marcantel, Judge Ned Doucet, Dave Johnson, Louis Koerner, Marie Breaux, Val Exnicios, Mark Babineaux, Frank Neuner, Patrick O'Keefe, Chris Goudeau and Wendy Tate, members of the executive committee of the Francophone Section of the Louisiana State Bar Association.

One of the best prerequisites of researching history is that it gave me the opportunity to visit Canada, my ancestral home. Since my first visit in 1989, I have made many friends who have provided me with warm hospitality and support, including Pierre Richard, Viola LeBreton Frigault, Charles Gaudet, Marc Belliveau, Maurice Crosby, Jean Gaudet, Dr. Jean-Douglas Comeau, Dominique Godbout, Gerard Johnson, Michel Cyr, Jean-Luc Chaisson, Dominique LeBlanc, Senator Gerald Comeaux, Guy Richard, Aurora Comeau, Michel Doucet, Yvon Fontaine, Stéphane Bergeron, Maurice Basque, Richard Laurin, Vaugh Madden, Georgette LeBlanc, André Fourcier, Romeo LeBlanc, Linda Fourcier,Valerie Roy, Neil Boucher, Jean-Marie Nadeau, Phil Comeau,

Michael Doucette, Judge Michel Bastarache and Paul Surette. *Merci, mes amis.*

My parents, Henry Lolly and Ella Mae Broussard Perrin, siblings Terry and Natial, and my children, Rebecca, Andy and Bruce, were always very supportive of my work and decision to proceed with the Petition to obtain an apology for the Acadian exile. Thank you very much. Special *grand merci* to Jean-Robert Frigault, former Director of Canadian/Acadian Affairs for CODOFIL, who encouraged me for thirteen years and helped to arrange the special meeting with the *Société Nationale de l'Acadie*, which led to the merging of our efforts. But the person who endured more, edited manuscripts, stayed with the children when I went to Canada or France and gave me the daily encouragement that I needed was my loving wife, Mary Leonise Broussard Perrin. I could not envision this book without Mary's help. With her, life is wonderful. I will always be very grateful to her.

Warren A. Perrin

DEDICATION

To my loving wife, Mary Leonise Broussard Perrin, who encouraged me to follow my instincts and immerse myself in our Acadian heritage.

EDITOR'S NOTES

For two centuries, the collective consciousness of the exiles pined for a grand hero, someone of their own cultural identification with the charismatic stature of Lee, Washington, Napoleon, El Cid or Alexander the Great. In the beginning they had many heroes and knew them quite personally, but the distances of time and geography, continuous ethnic persecution by humiliation and fragmented isolation had eroded their history. There was also, apparently, a reluctance to remember. Perhaps the past was just too painful, each successive present too tense with difficulty and the only goal for the future – one of simple survival. Whatever the cause, in Louisiana, where a large number of the disposed settled, the paucity of written or oral history or even folksongs pertaining to the aftermath of the Great Upheaval was astounding.

Then, in the 1940's, a global upheaval even greater than the distant event that had dispersed their ancestors to the far corners of two hemispheres unexpectedly landed many of them in a homeland at least twice removed. It was World War II and they were in France. There, they found newborn value in something they had that is very old, something that is basic for the survival of any culture and essential for any occupying power to abolish for lasting domination. It was their language. They still spoke French.

The Americans – it was still common at home in Louisiana to differentiate those who spoke only English from those who spoke French as 'American' of a different sort, a ruling caste – needed them for communication, this time, with people they were liberating. Ironically, the language faced with obliteration at home suddenly made them vital to the war effort overseas. And they discovered that their colloquial idiom wasn't as substandard as they had been led to believe, either. This was the genesis of the Acadian Renaissance. It all had to do with long-lost pride.

Two decades later, with the founding of the Council for the Development of French in Louisiana (CODOFIL), a cultural wildfire swept southern Louisiana. Contacts were established with long-lost cousins in faraway places and their respective, receptive governments, too. Special curricula were inaugurated at every educational level to teach a language and a history that previously had been at best ignored and ridiculed and at worst condemned and demeaned. The more they learned, the more they wanted to know. The search for the great hero had begun.

Among their cousins in Canada whose forebears had managed to remain, however, the story was quite different. After decades of hide-and-seek harassment by their oppressors, Acadians were finally allowed to resettle. Largely as the result of the continued militancy of their separatist neighbors, the Quebecois, successive governments acceded to their bilingualism, acquiesced to their passion for continued cultural identification. They had always known their grand hero. His name was Joseph *dit Beausoliel* Broussard. In fact, it would have been difficult to forget him partly because he was still being vilified as a bandit and a thug by the Canadian ruling caste, a situation similar to that of the memory of Emiliano Zapata in Mexico.

There were a couple of problems involved in the rediscovery of the true nature of this particular hero. The first and most obvious was that the scattered descendants of the exiles were not communicating. This would end with CODOFIL's establishment in 1968. The second and more lasting is that the hero left no written record of himself. A lot was written and rumored, continues to be written and rumored about what he did but not about what he thought, felt, or valued personally. Undoubtedly this was because he was a man of action and not words. While others talked the talk, he galloped the walk.

With sparse or no personal memoir, there is an irresistible invitation to speculate on motivation, vision of victory, personal judgment of success as opposed to failure, strategy underlying battlefield tactics or even the basic qualities of the individual's personality, morality and physical appearance. In short, there is a tendency to romanticize doers more than thinkers because there's just less to go on. There is a huge blank canvas begging for paint. Now, the rumors and inventions are making their way into print.

A good example of this is the depiction of him by Quebecoise and Acadian descendant Antoinine Maillet in her excellent, funny, sad, and generally beautiful novel *Pélagie-la-charrette* (*Pélagie of the Cart*), about the journey of a motley group of Acadian exiles and others picked up along the way from Georgia back to Canada overland in the first years after the mid-eighteenth Century deportations. The famous Acadian freedom fighter makes a cameo appearance in the narrative and Maillet blithely knocks at least twenty years off his age, ignores the man's wife and numerous children, restores his sexual virility and remakes him into the lost lover of the protagonist. This is the way legends have been born across all the ages.

There is such a thing as poetic (in this case novelistic) license. In the realm of art, anything goes and that is the way it should be. The problem occurs when people start investing art with reality. While myths may be fun, they obscure the truth. Broussard is the quintessential Acadian hero and thereby fair game for the imagination. In his case, the facts of his life need no elaboration to inspire. They are just not always as pretty as admirers would prefer.

Anyone who reads Warren Perrin's factual account of his ancestor's life, exploits and lasting influence will immediately understand why. But unless the reader has also examined some of the fictional representations of the valiant, violent, indefatigable résistance fighter or listened to some of the fanciful folktales told about him he may not be able to understand fully the enormous fascination for this figure among Acadians and the non-Acadian admirers of Cajun food, music and *joie de vivre* throughout the world. Cajuns don't laugh and sing and dance because that is all they know. Rather, they laugh and sing and dance because they've had hard lessons on how valuable it is to truly, fully simply live. Also, they feel they've earned the right to enjoy it.

"Lâche pas la patate," they say, "Don't drop the potato." Life may be a hot potato but they feel they can't drop it because it may turn out to be all they have to eat.

Beausoleil had every opportunity to learn this. He was – and continues to be in the cultural consciousness – an example of a man who lost a war, lost a homeland, lost much of his extended family to estrangement and death and was literally destroyed by exile in a physical way. He was forced into an environment where a disease (yellow fever) which was nonexistent in his homeland, thus providing him no natural resistance, periodically sliced through the countryside with the sickle of death. It was a horrid death, too. Victims often vomited black, congealed blood and bled from their eyes. And yet, after all the suffering and numerous defeats, somehow through his progeny eventually he won.

One of those descendants is Perrin. In fact, he is directly descended on both his mother's and his father's side of the family. He is fond of saying that this genetic concentration makes him "double trouble." The British knew that apparently genetic propensity for confrontation in *Beausoleil* and they now know that about Perrin. After a long campaign, Perrin extracted an apology from the British Crown for the deportations.

The real beauty of this record presented by Perrin, with newly discovered accounts of his ancestor's exploits, is the scarcity of speculation or elaboration. If you must achieve some concept of *Beausoleil* the man as opposed to *Beausoleil* the grand hero, you might examine some of his descendants. It is as good a method as any and better than most.

Chris Segura
Romancier, journaliste
Et descendant de Beausoleil

FOREWORD

Three years before the English founded the Jamestown colony, sixteen years before the *Mayflower* landed at Plymouth Rock, and seventeen years before the Dutch founded New Amsterdam, French pioneers established Acadia. The year was 1604. If, by historical accident, the English colonies of New Brunswick, Prince Edward Island, and Nova Scotia had joined with their fellow colonists in the thirteen southern English colonies in the War of the American Revolution, today they would probably be part of the United States. Thus, the first Thanksgiving would not have taken place in Massachusetts but in Nova Scotia, and the Pilgrims would be replaced by Acadians. And, Americans interested in promoting their family pedigree would say that their ancestors came over on the *Le Jonas* instead of the *Mayflower*.

In 2004, Acadians the world over celebrated the 400th anniversary of the genesis of our people, our culture, and our history in North America. Of course, our Acadian roots are in France, but it was only after 1604 that a people known as Acadians (and later as Cajuns in Louisiana) emerged. There can be no better time than this anniversary and celebration for Warren Perrin to pen his excellent study of a great Acadian, Joseph *dit Beausoleil* Broussard (b.1702-d.1765).

It is said that extraordinary times produce extraordinary people. That was certainly the case with *Beausoleil*. But to say that the *Grand Dérangement* was an extraordinary time is an understatement – a gross understatement. It is one of the darkest chapters in North American history in that it represents the first – and perhaps the only – example of ethnic cleansing of Europeans in the history of the continent. Beginning in 1755 and ending in 1763, British and New England militia cleared Acadia of Acadians. It is impossible to capture in words the agony, the pain, the suffering, and the humiliation of the Acadian people during the years of expulsion, exile, homelessness, and wandering. Thousands of Acadians died of smallpox, dysentery, scurvy, and malnutrition on overcrowded and under rationed British ships. Thousands more were imprisoned in England and in Nova Scotia. Yet, despite insurmountable odds, the Acadians fought back, and *Beausoleil* Broussard was their leader.

Centuries later, modernity would call *Beausoleil* Broussard's tactics guerilla warfare. *Beausoleil* simply called it *la guerre* (the war). He was a brave man, but his fighters – farmers, fishermen and trappers – armed with agricultural implements, homemade knives, swords – and an occasional rifle – were no match for the army and navy of the British Empire. He and his family spent the last years of *Le Grand Dérangement* under heavy guard in a Halifax prison. Perhaps it was his love of liberty; perhaps it was his unquenchable desire to escape British rule; perhaps it was a combination of the two; but when the French and Indian War ended and he and his family were released from prison, he led his people to a New Acadia.

Dr. William Arceneaux,
President
La Fondation CODOFIL

INTRODUCTION

The central concept of this book is basically an examination of the life of one man who has become a mythical folk hero to people of Acadian decent, both in Acadia and in south Louisiana: Joseph *dit Beausoleil* Broussard. *Beausoleil* was a man of French descent who was born in 1702 in Acadie, an area that is now the Canadian Province of Nova Scotia. Coming down to us through the pages of history, as well as in folklore and oral tradition, he appears to have been a colorful, enigmatic and charismatic man, a revolutionary whom the British characterized as a rogue and an outlaw. As a young man, *Beausoleil* consorted with the aboriginal Mi'Kmaq of the area, with whom he was on good terms, although forbidden by British law to do so. In his early twenties he was accused of having fathered a child out of wedlock and was involved in various other civil disputes. Later, he engaged in physical fights with neighbors over ownership of a certain parcel of land.

To the Acadians then and now, however, *Beausoleil* is revered as a patriot. Unlike many other Acadians who chose to accept their fate, that of forcible exile by the British, *Beausoleil*, who had learned much about aboriginal warfare tactics from his good friends the Mi'Kmaq, decided to fight. In 1763, after the majority of the Acadians had already been deported, Governor Wilmot offered the Acadians still remaining in Nova Scotia, including *Beausoleil* and his troublesome rag-tag band of guerilla fighters, the opportunity to stay and become "good British subjects," provided they took the Oath of Allegiance to the British Crown. Many accepted the offer, however, *Beausoleil* refused to do so. Why? Perhaps it was due in part to his obstreperous personality or to his training with the Mi'Kmaq, but more likely it was due to his passion for his Acadian heritage. *Beausoleil* was a descendant of the first Europeans who had left feudalism and oppression behind to forge a newfound freedom and identity in this place called Acadie. That identity, inherited from his ancestors, represented the years of struggle that they had experienced in order to give *Beausoleil* and his children the opportunity to live in a land free of servitude to tyrannical governments where they could live in peace and practice their own religion. We can never know for sure what motivated him, but we do know that the result of his efforts allowed the Acadian culture to continue developing in a new environment. After he ended his fight with the British, *Beausoleil* led many of his people to

Louisiana's bayou country, allowing those Acadians to live in peace and community once again and to maintain their cultural identity. This identity continued to evolve as a vibrant part of the American mosaic.

Likewise, my husband and *Beausoleil* descendant, Warren Perrin, is a man blessed with his ancestor's enduring tenacity and passion for protecting his Acadian community. Using his pen and legal training as his rifle, Perrin decided to bring the work that *Beausoleil* started two centuries before to a final conclusion. His Petition to correct misconceptions about Acadian history – and to clear *Beausoleil*'s name – resulted in a Royal Proclamation, an acknowledgement by Queen Elizabeth II of the wrongs committed against the Acadian people during their deportation. The Proclamation stands as a redemption for all Acadian people, and for *Beausoleil* in particular.

Both Warren and *Beausoleil* were presented with opportunities and challenges that they chose to accept: *Beausoleil* to wage a battle against the British to protect his community of Acadians with all the cunning and strength he could muster; Warren to wage a legal battle with the British with all of the intelligence and diplomacy he possessed to correct history's misconceptions about the Acadian people, and to put an end at last to the exile.

After studying Acadian history, Warren came to the realization that there were legal procedures he could use to correct the historical record concerning his ancestors. He was not an artist, writer, musician, or military person – he was a lawyer. Therefore, he used those skills and life's training to attack, some would say with great militancy, those historical perspectives concerning the Acadians that have come to be referred to as "dead certainties." By taking this risk of challenging history, Warren did not miss the opportunity to do as *Beausoleil* had done to grant to his own descendants the opportunity to be proud to be part of this hard-won legacy called Acadian culture.

At the beginning of this undertaking, I asked my husband why he wanted to write this book. Why a book on *Beausoleil?* His answer was that he questioned the accuracy of the pro-British historian's conclusion that the Acadians as a whole were a rebellious, belligerent, and quarrelsome people during the pre-dispersal period at which time they were considered British subjects. If the British declared the Acadians "rebels," or enemies of the state, they could be subjected under British law to loss of their rights and thence to deportation. With this in mind, Warren decided to take a critical, detailed, and objective look at Acadian history to see if the official interpretations justifying the Acadian deportation would stand up to scrutiny. He also wanted to research the life of *Beausoleil,* the man always held up to have been the leader or scoundrel of the insurrection to see what part he played in these events. Although we know he was extremely anti-British and had a contentious, militant character, one must conclude by the sheer number of Acadian descendants in Louisiana today that his life's ultimate struggle did, in the end, merit him the distinction of being the foremost champion of the Acadian culture. Still, one also learns that, as with all human beings, *Beausoleil* was not a perfect individual. Moreover, like many other significant historical icons, he set out to accomplish one thing and ended up accomplishing something far more positive. This book examines both the positive and negative actions of *Beausoleil* and concludes that his true character lies somewhere in between; that is, he was not necessarily always a righteous, upstanding pillar of the Acadian community, but neither was he the murderous blackguard the British made him out to be.

The next question I remember thinking was this: from our vantage point in the twenty-first century, what did *Beausoleil* actually accomplish? At what cost? And how and why did he become such a folk hero? Knowing the bits and pieces of his life's story, it is apparent that *Beausoleil* was capable of making harmful life decisions. It appears that revenge was his motivation in the beginning for leading the resistance against the British. Revenge may, at times, be a natural human response to certain situations, but it is not a positive motivation. Because of his tenacity, many of his decisions resulted in the tragic loss of the lives of family members and fellow insurgents. Toward the end of his military efforts against the British, when he must have finally realized the fruitlessness of continuing his resistance – after even France itself gave up the fight – only then did he set about uniting Acadian families and preparing to depart from his beloved homeland to what he hoped would be a better life in a new Acadia.

Both *Beausoleil* and Warren Perrin were searching for resolution – and perhaps both men finally found it: *Beausoleil* in his new homeland in Louisiana, Warren in Canada with the Royal Proclamation. *Beausoleil* would have been proud.

The first part of this book defines the society into which *Beausoleil* was born and speaks of his early life events and his militant struggles with the British who had for years wanted to lay claim to the Acadians' rich and profitable lands. Subsequent chapters discuss his epic odyssey during which *Beausoleil* led a group of one hundred ninety-three Acadians to Louisiana, the New Acadia, with the hope that his beloved Acadian culture would survive. The last half of the book discusses the repercussions of his life that ultimately led an eighth generation descendant of *Beausoleil*, Warren Perrin, to begin a legal action called the Petition. This petition was resolved by the signing of the Royal Proclamation on December 9, 2003.

Mary Leonise Broussard Perrin

PART I
ACADIAN ODYSSEY

Louisiana artist Robert Dafford's painting of "Beausoleil" on display at the Acadian Museum.

CHAPTER 1
THE FIRST BROUSSARD IN ACADIA

Three decades before he would become the father of the most famous, and, by most accounts, the most ferocious freedom-fighter in French Canada, François Brossard paid a widow for the clothes of her drowned husband René Bonnin, a trapper. It was an obscure yet poignant moment in the history of the struggling colony known then as Acadia, or, in French, Acadie. Nothing could be wasted in the new colony. Sentiment gave way to the practical. Sudden death was common. Survival was the ultimate prize and it was won by the strong, the lucky, the clever, and, most of all, the determined.

The purchase of the clothes was documented by Acadian geneologist, Stephen White, *Centre d'etudes acadiennes* at the University of Moncton, New Brunswick. This transaction confirms that François was in Acadie as early as February 3, 1672.

It was an epoch and a way of life similar to that of upstate New York as depicted by James Fenimore Cooper in *The Last of the Mohicans.* Shortly, by historical measure, Acadie would become embroiled in the same international conflict of that historical novel. However, the Acadian story concluded with unimaginably tragic results. Acadia was only sixty-seven years in existence when Brossard bought a dead man's clothes. Although there had already been hostilities between the colony and neighboring British settlers, François Brossard had no way of knowing that the community, as he knew it, would crumble only eighty-four years later. With the colony nearly at the halfway point between its founding and its disaster, he had yet to marry, much less conceive either his famous sons or the events that would transpire to displace his progeny halfway across the North American continent and into history and legend.

On June 26, 1604, Pierre Dugua, Samuel de Champlain and seventy-seven other men had arrived at ill-fated St. Croix Island (now on the U.S.-Canadian border in Maine) to carve out the first French settlement in North America. Dugua, a nobleman known as Sieur de Monts, is remembered for besting the English in establishing a settlement in North America.[1] Dugua sailed with two galleons into Passamaquoddy Bay and up a river to an island that appeared defensible and well-suited to his planned settlement. Armed with a grant from the king of France, his mission was to colonize the land and bring Christianity to its inhabitants. Dugua named the island St. Croix because it was near the confluence of rivers resembling the arms of a cross.

The settlers cleared a site, erected dwellings, a kitchen, storehouse, blacksmith shop and chapel, and planted gardens. In early October, 1604, not long after Champlain returned from a historic voyage to Mount Desert Island, the first snow fell, setting the stage for an unusually harsh winter. By Christmas, the river was choked with ice floes, cutting off access to the mainland. The settlers ran low on drinking water, fresh food and firewood. They developed scurvy, surviving on preserved food, wine and melted snow. Thirty-five of the men died and were buried on the island. After a supply ship arrived in June, Dugua dismantled the settlement and moved it to Nova Scotia at a spot Champlain named Port Royal.

French colonists were sent to Acadie on orders of King Henry IV of France. The 1604 settlement came three years before English colonists landed in Jamestown and sixteen years before the Pilgrims sailed the Mayflower to Plymouth, Massachusetts. They began to settle and cultivate the land to develop a foothold for France's first settlement in North America. Though Acadia was small, it was strategically important because it lay close to New England, the mouth of the St. Lawrence River, and the North Atlantic fishing banks.[2] In 1632, Cardinal Richelieu, Minister to King Louis XIII, organized the departure to Acadia of French families of diverse origins and professions.

In 1678, François Brossard, the first known Brossard in Acadie, married Catherine Richard (daughter of Michel and Madeline Richard) and followed his friend Pierre Thibaudot to settle the hamlet of Chipoudie (now known as Hopewell Hill, New Brunswick) in what was then considered mainland Acadie near the Petitcoudiac River.[3] Eleven children were born of their marriage:[4] Madeleine (b. 1681, married Pierre Landry); Pierre (b. 1684, married Marguerite Bourg); Marie Anne (b. 1686, married Rene Pierre "dit Laverduke" Doucet); Catherine (b. 1690, married Charles Landry); Elizabeth (b. 1693, married Pierre Bourg); François (b. 1694); Claude (b. 1695, married Anne Babin); Françoise (b. 1697); Alexandre (b. 1699, married Marguerite Thibodeaux); Joseph *dit Beausoleil* (b. 1702, married Agnès Thibodeaux) and Jean Baptiste (b. 1703, married Cecile Babin).[5]

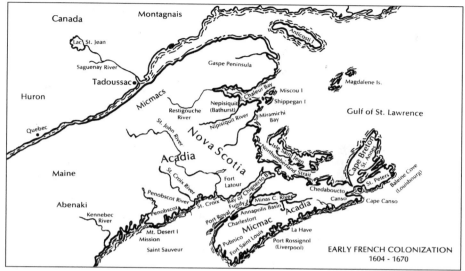

Source: Trenholm, Norden and Trenholm, *A History of Fort Lawrence*
by (Sherwood Printing Ltd. 1985).

Later, the family returned to live in Port Royal, Acadie. However, two of his sons, Joseph *dit Beausoleil* and Alexandre, remained and established their residences at Chipoudie on land that had been granted to their wives, the granddaughters of Pierre Thibaudot (Thibodeau). Later, Alexandre settled at Petitcoudiac, a village founded by Guillaume Blanchard. *Beausoleil* took up residence farther north at Le Cran (now known as Stoney Creek, New Brunswick).

As the Acadian communities grew, the settlers traded their surplus crops with British colonists from nearby New England in exchange for much-needed manufactured goods.[6] They often had to resort to smuggling in order to avoid provoking the French and British authorities who competed for their loyalties. Acadians were known as family-loving farmers who followed pastoral pursuits and maintained a relatively isolated existence.

The Acadians got along well with the native people, particularly the Mi'Kmaq.[7] These aboriginal people taught the colonists the rudiments of survival in this land and played a crucial role in the settlement of Acadia.[8] They showed the settlers where to hunt and introduced them to edible and medicinal plants. Without the help and friendship of the Mi'Kmaq, the Acadians would have had little hope of survival. The

3

origin of the name of the colony is in fact believed by some linguists to come from the Mi'Kmaq word *"cadique,"* meaning a good place to camp or settle. Remarkably, the Mi'Kmaq saved some French colonists from starving one winter by inviting the settlers to live with them. The two peoples maintained a rigorous and flourishing trade in furs, the basis of the early colony's economy. The Mi'Kmaq and Acadians developed intertwined links through marriages, mutually sustained admiration, and protective alliances.[9]

Early in his life, François came to be known by the British as a dissident. About 1713, shortly after Nova Scotia became a British possession, he was imprisoned along with four other Acadians from Port Royal. This was a gesture of retribution by the newly-arrived British authorities for the seizing of a British soldier by an Acadian, Abraham Gaudet. Although François was liberated from confinement shortly thereafter, he remained fiercely anti-British for the rest of his life. His militancy and hatred of the British profoundly influenced his children – particularly *Beausoleil.*

According to church records, François Brossard died unexpectedly on December 31, 1716, without receiving the final sacraments of the Catholic Church. Although there are no records for substantiation, it is believed that his wife Catherine Richard died in the late 1750s at an advanced age during the tumultuous period known as *le Grand Dérangement,* or the Acadian exile, which commenced in 1755.[10]

CHAPTER 2
THE EARLY YEARS: COLONIZATION

During the 150-year period that Acadie was in existence, it was the subject of many military campaigns. The colony changed hands at least eight times between the British and the French. The first British attack on the Acadians occurred in July, 1613, followed by another attack in 1619. The hegemonic British were based in what is now known as the state of Virginia. In 1654, British colonists led another attack. Realizing that Acadie represented a strategic geographic area situated at the entrance to the St. Lawrence River - believed to be important to the development of an empire in North America - the British government conceived of an idea to deport the Acadians from Acadie as early as 1650.

The Brossard brothers, Alexandre and Joseph, were both sometimes called *Beausoleil* after their small native village near Port Royal. Some contend that the name, meaning "beautiful sun," refers to the way daylight sparkles on the rippling water of a nearby stream. Since both brothers played major roles in the effort to prevent the deportation of the Acadians by the British, the exploits of each were sometimes confused by their common nickname.[11]

The path that the name "Brossard" took to the spelling "Broussard" was similar to that of a meandering river. Many Acadian surnames have undergone remarkable spelling changes in the centuries since Acadia was established. Most often these changes were instituted by the pen strokes of officials foreign to the culture. The British changed the original "Brossard" to "Brussard" and alternately back to "Brossard" or "Broussard" apparently at the whim of the writer. It survives today in Louisiana as "Broussard," and is used here after throughout the narrative except when a different spelling is included in historical quotations. Joseph *dit Beausoleil* Broussard was born in 1702 at Port Royal (Annapolis Royal, Nova Scotia). On September 11, 1725, at Annapolis Royal, Broussard married Agnès, the daughter of Michel Thibodeau (Thibodeaux) and Agnès Dugas, one of the most influential Acadian families at that time. In 1727, they settled at Chipoudie (New Brunswick)[12] along with his brother Alexandre, who married Agnès' sister, Marguerite, in 1724.

For thirty years they lived a life of relative peace in the area of what is present-day Moncton, New Brunswick, on the Petitcoudiac River. Joseph and Agnès had eleven children: Victor-Gregoire, Raphael, Claude, Thimothee, Isabelle, Joseph Gregory, Amand, Jean Gregory, Marguerite, Françoise and François. Like many Acadians, they engaged in the unique method of reclaiming land from the sea by draining marsh lands and building dikes. The work was done on the Petitcoudiac River by employing an Acadian specialty of trapping river bottom sediment in marshy areas. Taking advantage of what scientists tell us are the highest tides on earth, Acadians built dikes intermittently fitted with one-way sluices that trapped muddy water at high tide and allowed water to drain away at low tide. In this way, they actually created their own fertile farmland. An irony of history is that by this enterprise the Acadians created the very farmland that the British coveted enough to plot their expulsion. In a sense, the Acadian ingenuity for survival helped bring about their destruction. This was accomplished on the Petitcoudiac River, which is a tidal river. A British soldier described *Beausoleil's* settlement on the Petitcoudiac River:

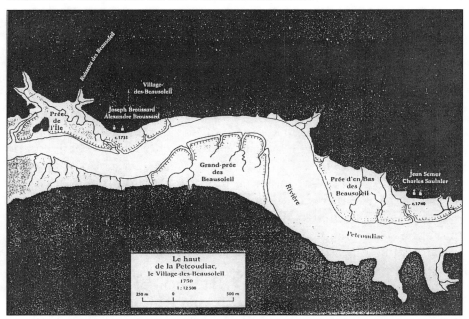

Source: Paul Surette, *La prée de l'Ille et le Village-des-Beausoleil, Atlas de L'Etablissement des Acadiens,* 1660–1785. Note: This map shows the location of *Beausoleil's* village. Two white dots in the upper left-hand quadrant indicate the actual dwellings of *Beausoleil* and Alexandre.

The river extends far into the wilderness and, by means of certain portages, almost to Quebec. Our couriers and travelers take this route to Quebec, a distance estimated at about 160 leagues. It is 30 leagues from here to the mouth of the river but the distance can be reduced by going overland. This is by way of Pekoudiac [*sic*], where the *Beausoleils* live, who grew rich, so it is said, on the spoil taken from the English during the last war. They behave like the Indians, with whom they are on very intimate terms. [13]

Beausoleil traded with the Mi'Kmaq, and he became very close to the aboriginal people.[14] He learned to speak their language and many of them learned to communicate in his. The British became paranoid of the Acadian's relationship with the Mi'Kmaq. In 1722, the British issued a proclamation prohibiting the entertaining of Mi'Kmaq by Acadians. Captain Hussey, a British officer, wrote:

There are two families on the upper Petkoudiac [*sic*], named *Beausoleil*, who, though they are not Indians, live as they do. Moses has enjoined them to watch the movements of the English. These *Beausoleils* enriched themselves during the recent disorders, and boast that they did much damage to the English and took from them property of value and many cattle. They speak the language of the Indians and obtain from them all the beaver skins which Moses sells.[15]

The early years that *Beausoleil* and Agnès shared together were a time of relative calm, punctuated by the trials of colonial life. It stands in stark contrast to the tumultuous years to follow.

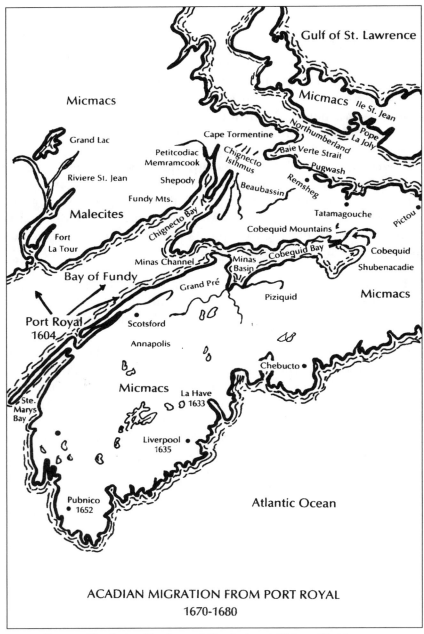

Gulf of St. Lawrence

Micmacs

Micmacs Ile St. Jean

Pope
La Joly

Grand Lac

Cape Tormentine

Northumberland

Baie Verte Strait

Petitcodiac
Memramcook

Chignecto
Isthmus

Pugwash

Riviere St. Jean

Shepody

Beaubassin

Remsheg

Fundy Mts.

Malecites

Chignecto Bay

Tatamagouche

Pictou

Fort
La Tour

Cobequid Mountains

Cobequid

Minas Channel

Cobequid Bay

Minas
Basin

Shubenacadie

Bay of Fundy

Grand Pré

Piziquid

Micmacs

Port Royal
1604

Scotsford

Annapolis

Chebucto

Ste.
Marys
Bay

Micmacs

La Have
1633

Liverpool
1635

Pubnico
1652

Atlantic Ocean

ACADIAN MIGRATION FROM PORT ROYAL
1670-1680

Source: Trenholm, Norden and Trenholm, *A History of Fort Lawrence*
by (Sherwood Printing Ltd. 1985).

CHAPTER 3
BEAUSOLEIL'S FOUR CIVIL DISPUTES

Colonial records show that Acadians had major civil disputes. This is palpably demonstrated by the four claims brought against *Beausoleil* before he had reached the age of twenty-five years: assault and battery, consorting with the Indians, a land dispute and a paternity claim. Clearly, these disputes with his fellow Acadians and the British authorities provide insight into his character. At a young age, *Beausoleil* was a man who stirred controversy and yet he could be accommodating. He was becoming just the type of person who would stand up to the British army, at that time the most powerful military force in the world.

Historian John B. Brebner wrote that the bringing of civil suits was sometimes a form of amusement for the Acadians: "pioneer communities' court costs are small and going to law is often a sort of social diversion." [16] More often, however, disputes were settled outside of the law by community consensus. The Acadians had established a strong social cohesion. According to Brebner, "a clan, a body of people united by blood ties, common beliefs and common aims for the group as a whole ...." [17]

The solidarity of the early Acadian settlers was exhibited when a relatively new arrival, Louis Thibault, brought charges against *Beausoleil* for harassing and threatening him. Since Thibault was not part of the established Acadian community, but rather a newcomer and an outsider, he did not pursue the normal course of settling disputes within the family. Instead, he filed a complaint with the British authorities who summoned *Beausoleil* to appear before them to answer the charges "for maltreatment and using (Thibault) unjustly." This charge was filed with the General Court at Annapolis Royal. On August 10, 1724, Lieutenant Governor Doucett ordered *Beausoleil* to appear and served notice upon him to appear; but *Beausoleil* refused to accept the order, and he reportedly physically abused the process server: "And that Whereas Said Tibeau (Thibault) had Again Returned and Made Oath that when he went to Deliver him the Orders, that he not only beat him, but he took the Orders and Despitefully Throw [*sic*] them on the Ground."

Beausoleil failed to appear. On August 12, Doucett issued a new order and added charges that he had consorted with the Mi'Kmaq who had attacked the British Garrison at Annapolis Royal. *Beausoleil* finally appeared to answer all charges. However, he sought a pardon: "presented [Doucett] with a Petition being pardon and Confessing to the Cause of the Concealing the late Affairs of the Indians." After *Beausoleil's* interrogation he was arrested and imprisoned: "Abusing Louis Tibeau [Thibault] and Contempt of Orders, was put Prisoner upon Guard." The British authorities did not have sufficient forces to keep the Acadians "under due subjection," so a compromise was reached:

> It was Judged proper to Answer the Deputees, That the Governor and Council, purely in consideration to them for Having Done their Duty in bringing them [*les accusés*] to the Governor, and not Doubting but that they Would according to their promises faithfully Discharge the Trust of Deputees, and by their Vigilence prevent all Such Disorders in the Government for the future ...

About the same time, *Beausoleil* was also charged by the British authorities with consorting with the Indians and not disclosing to the authorities the activities of the Mi'Kmaq in the area. The "Broussard Affair" shows that the established Acadian society, or the entrenched Acadian families, protected their own to the detriment of new arrivals. In 1724, Louis Thibault was not able to show that he was part of the established community and therefore he did not attain the full results of his plea. However, he did achieve partial success because Broussard was imprisoned for a short time and humiliated within the community. Thereafter, Broussard was considered by the British to be a "suspect individual."

In 1725, while the Thibaudot (Thibodeaux) clan was attempting to re-establish itself at Chipoudie, the husbands of the two oldest daughters of Michel Thibaudot, the feisty brothers Alexandre and *Beausoleil*, were determined to fix the territorial limits in the area called Anse des Demoiselles, where the two sons of Jacques Leger and others had performed some settlement work.[18] The Broussard brothers laid claim to the land on the basis that their father-in-law was one of the first, if not the very first, to claim the marsh in the area. The Broussard brothers warned against anyone attempting to invade the "réserve Thibaudot."

10

This document is a record of the baptism of Marguerite Tibodeau, daughter of Michel Tibodeau and Agnes Dugas. Following is a typewritten transcript in French:

Ce seizieme de may de l'annee mil sept cent six moy soussigne faisant les fonction curiales ay fayte les ceremonies de bapteme a Marguerite Tibodeau Fille de Michel Tibodeau et de Agnes Dugas legitimement conjoins, elle est nee le 22 decembre et elle a ete ondoyee par Jeanne LeBreton parce que la rayson de froid l'a empeche d'etre amenee a l'eglise.

Elle a eu pour parrain Claude Tibodeau et pour marraine Francoise Comeau En foy de quoi j'ai signe avec le parrain et la marraine le meme jour et an que dessus.

s/Clode Tibeaudeau   X marque de la marraine
s/ F. Justinien Durant Recollett Missionaire

Following is the English translation of this document:

This sixteenth day of May of the year one thousand seven hundred and six, I the undersigned fulfilling my pastoral duties have performed the ceremony of baptism for Marguerite Tibodeau daughter of Michel Tibodeau and of Agnes Dugas legally conjoined (married) she was born 22 December and she was privately baptized by Jeanne LeBreton because cold temperature prevented her from being brought to the church.

She had as Godfather Claude Tibodeau and as Godmother Francoise Comeau. In good faith I have signed with the Godfather and Godmother this Same day and year indicated above.

(continued next page)

Reproduction and translation of the baptism record of Marguerite Tibodeau (1706)

Interpretation by Dick Thibodeau:

Michel Tibodeau, born 1678, was the 12th child, and 5th son, born to Pierre and Jeanne Theriot following Pierre the younger who was born 1676. Michel married Agnes Dugas on 13 Nov 1704. His brother Claude, who served as Godfather, was born 1684, which made him 21 years old at time of the baptism. Michel was 26 when he married. Interesting to note that many men seemed to marry later and most girls seemed to marry younger. Agnes Dugas was 19 at the time she married Michel.

Saint-Jean-Baptiste de Port Royal was the name of the parish that ministered to the Acadian population of the area at that time. I am sure that the church was located in the Port Royal Village. The Tibodeau establishment was located some 11 miles up the Port Royal River, then known as *Rivere du Dauphin* by the French. (That translates to "River of the Dolphin".) The original parish registers are today located at the Provincial Archives of Nova Scotia in Halifax. There are of course copies located in other Provincial Archives. I got this one in Trois Rivieres, Quebec.

The baptism record indicates that it was too cold to bring the child to the church for the official ceremony, therefore, Jeanne LeBreton, who may have been the mid-wife, baptized her temporarily. It was not to be until the 16th of May before she would be officially baptized by the Missionary Recollett Priest. It would appear that the winters were brutal. The name Jeanne LeBreton was most difficult to read and all four of us working on this document, Roger, his wife Pierrette, myself and my wife, Therese, were not really able to make it out. I finally determined that it was Jeanne LeBreton because of the way the priest made the letter "B" in the word Decembre and then looked in the census of 1714 and saw that there was listed in Port Royal a "LeBreton and wife" with no first names shown. That seemed enough evidence to feel fairly certain that it could very well be Jeanne LeBreton. This was not one of the more important elements of the baptismal record. Another item in this document which was very problematic (and my wife Therese was the one to put out the first hint as to what it might be) was the word *Ondoyer* in French. She remembered the term from her growing up years in Quebec as indicating a child who was baptized at birth because of some urgency such as possibly dying before getting to a priest. She could not remember the exact spelling but it was enough for Roger and Pierrette to take it from there. The term *Ondoyer* means, in a sense, to anoint with water which is what the baptism process involves. A French term relative to this is used for flooding, *inondation* for those amongst you who speak French.

Marguerite was the first child born to Michel and Agnes Dugas. There were to be fourteen more to follow, a family of 15 children. Is it any wonder there are so many Thibodeaus today? Marguerite would marry Alexandre Brossard 7 Feb 1724. The next child born, another girl by the name of Agnes, married Alexandre's brother Joseph Brossard who would become known as Joseph *dit Beausoleil* Brossard, probably the most well known and fiercest freedom fighter against the British of all the Acadians. His wife Agnes was, of course, the granddaughter of Pierre, our Ancestor. The Brossard family lived in Chipoudy.

The Broussard brothers moved their young families to the reclaimed area during the fall of 1727. Sometime thereafter, Jean Léger and Etienne Saulnier, who were engaged to the daughters of Abraham Comeaux, continued the work that they had undertaken in close proximity to the area then claimed by the Broussard brothers. The brothers once again strenuously opposed the presence of the Saulniers on "their land" and threatened to use force to ensure that others stayed away.

In a third dispute, the Broussard brothers also claimed the northern part of a river where the Saulniers had established their camp. They took aggressive action by leaving their land, assigning the responsibility of defending it to the oldest son of René Blanchard and claiming their rights to the land in front of the Saulniers. They claimed all of the marsh property located on the northern part of the Mi'Kmaq's camps, approximately 12 kilometers further. For the times, this was a bold move in the Acadian community.

The fourth major civil dispute involving *Beausoleil* occurred in 1726: *Beausoleil*, who had recently married, was accused of fathering an illegitimate child.[19] Although he denied the accusation, he was imprisoned for refusing to provide for the child's maintenance. The case: on May 12, 1726, His Majesty's Council at Annapolis Royal at Lieutenant Governor John Doucett's house was presented with a dispute regarding the "paternity" of an illegitimate child. Marie Daigle, wife of Jacques Goutille, asked the Council to declare that a married man, Joseph Broussard *dit Beausoleil*, husband of Agnès Thibodeaux, was the biological father of the child of her daughter Mary. Mrs. Daigle accused *Beausoleil* of "committing fornication with her daughter Mary who being brought to bed of a daughter had laid the same to the said Broussard, and he refusing the child maintenance and denying himself to be the father prayed relief." [20] *Beausoleil*, answering in his own defense to the charge, appeared before the Council declaring himself innocent, furthermore replying that he was "very innocent and not the father, having never had any carnal dealings with her." [21]

Mrs. Daigle acted as her daughter's representative before the Council of the Lieutenant Governor of Nova Scotia, represented by John Doucett. The midwife was put under oath and testified that when the girl was in her most violent pains of delivery, she declared that Joseph Broussard was the real father of her child. The Council ruled in favor of Mrs. Daigle and ordered *Beausoleil* to pay child support in the amount

Marriage Certificate
Joseph Broussard
and
Agnes Tibaudeau

On September 11, 1725, after publishing three announcements of the present marriage on August 26, and consecutively on September 7 and 8 of the present year and no impediment having presented itself, after securing the mutual consent of the two parties, I bestowed the nuptial blessing upon Joseph Broussard, 23 years of age, the son of the deceased François Broussard and of Catherine Richard on the one hand, and Agnes Tibaudeau, 19 years of age, daughter of Michel Tibaudeau and Agnes Dugast. The aforementioned marriage was performed in the presence of John Broussard, brother of the aforesaid groom, of Louis Fimard, son of Alexander Fimard, of Michel Tibaudeau, father of the aforesaid bride, of Claude Tibaudeau and of several other relatives and friends, all from Port Royal, who, having declared to the widow of [the brothers] Michel and Claude Tibeaudeau having received no money, signed with me.

Michel Tibeaudeaux

Claude Tibeaudeau

R. C. de B.

Translation of the marriage record of *Beausoleil* and Agnes Tibodeau (1725) of three shillings and nine pence per week until the child reached the age of eight years old. The court order also declared that he should immediately provide some good security for his faithful compliance with the order or go to prison until he could find security to put up. Abram [Abraham] Bourg, one of the deputies, and William Bourgeway [Bourgeois], local inhabitant, did come forward and engage themselves each in a hundred pound security bond for *Beausoleil's* punctual compliance with the Council's order.

Two months after the verdict, *Beausoleil's* mother, Catherine Richard, successfully appeared before the Council to request a reduction of Mary Daigle's child support to five shillings per month. Interestingly, Jeanne Dupuis, wife of Guillaume Blanchard, volunteered to care for the child for five shillings per month. More interestingly, Mary Daigle – faced with the possibility of losing her child – opted to keep her baby without receiving any child support from *Beausoleil*. Charles Landry, *Beausoleil's* brother-in-law, then offered to be answerable for the nursing of the baby and to give shelter to the mother for a period of one year. Landry's proposal was accepted by all.

Acadian historian and *Beausoleil* biographer Ronnie-Gilles LeBlanc surmises that the two civil claims brought against *Beausoleil* in 1724 and 1726 were probably responsible for his decision to leave his native hamlet and resettle his young family in the Chipoudie region on lands that had been claimed by his wife's family (Thibodeaux/Thibodeau). To so opine is mere conjecture because there is nothing but circumstantial evidence for the family's relocation.

The civil case offers a unique glimpse into the system which existed at the time to resolve disputes among Acadians. The involvement of so many persons in a private civil dispute, and the practical solution that apparently satisfied all those involved, demonstrates the cohesiveness which was then present in the early eighteenth-century Acadian community. Finally, it shows the influence and prestige which the women of Acadie had at the time: the intervention of *Beausoleil's* mother, Catherine Richard, as well as Marie Daigle and Jeanne Dupuis, strongly suggests that within the context of seventeenth- and eighteenth-century Acadia, women played major roles in all aspects of Acadian affairs – social, political and legal. *Beausoleil's* involvement in so many legal disputes at so young an age heralds the character of a man who would become, to the British view, an outlaw, murderer and pirate, and, to the

Acadians' view, a patriot and the "father of New Acadia."

Although his actions appeared to the British as troublesome, he could not sit quietly by and let those in authority have their way with the Acadian people and his Acadian homeland. *Beausoleil* was a man of action, one who thought of freedom as mankind's natural tendency, one who loathed oppression. In this respect, he could be compared with other contemporary figures in North American history, such as Thomas Jefferson, who may have also fathered a child out of wedlock, and who, tired of British oppression, led the American Colonies into a revolution against that government with a poorly trained and poorly equipped army. Both men shared the qualities of being passionate, somewhat elusive men of tantalizing inner complexity, whose aggressive actions drew formal rebukes from British authorities. Both men are revolutionaries who became cultural icons.

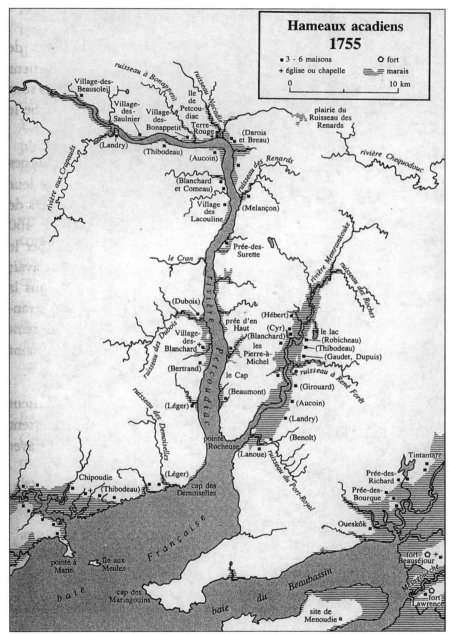

**Hameaux acadiens
1755**

■ 3 - 6 maisons   ○ fort
+ église ou chapelle   ≋ marais

0   10 km

ruisseau à Bonappetit

ruisseau Nacadie

Village-des-
Beausoleil

Village-
des-
Saulnier

Village-
des-
Bonappetit

île
de
Petcou-
diac
Terre-
Rouge

(Darois
et Breau)

plairie du
Ruisseau des
Renards

rivière Chequodouc

(Landry)

(Thibodeau)

(Aucoin)

rivière aux Crapauds

ruisseau des Renards

(Blanchard
et Comeau)

(Melançon)

Village
des
Lacouline

Prée-des-
Surette

rivière Menramkouke

ruisseau des Roches

le Cran

(Dubois)

ruisseau des Dubois

prée d'en
Haut

(Hébert)

(Cyr)

le lac

Village-
des-
Blanchard

(Blanchard)

les
Pierre-à-
Michel

(Robicheau)

(Thibodeau)

(Gaudet, Dupuis)

(Bertrand)

le Cap

ruisseau à René Forêt

(Léger)

(Beaumont)

(Girouard)

ruisseau des Demoiselles

(Aucoin)

(Landry)

pointe
Rocheuse

(Benoît)

Tintamare

(Lanoue)

ruisseau du Port-Royal

Prée-des-
Richard

Chipoudie

(Léger)

Prée-des-
Bourque

(Thibodeau)

cap des
Demoiselles

Oueskôk

Française

pointe à
Marie

île aux
Meules

fort
Beauséjour

baie

cap des
Maringouins

baie

du

Beaubassin

fort
Lawrence

site de
Menoudie

Source: Paul Surette, *Petcoudiac: Colonisation et destruction 1731 – 1755 (Les Editions d'Acadie,* 1988).
Note *Village-des-Beausoleil* at upper left.

CHAPTER 4
THE RESISTANCE

The geographic isolation of the Acadians living on the Petitcoudiac River left them relatively free of British domination. They became very independent and self-sufficient. This fostered a clannish society that developed its own unique culture. The only outsiders trusted by these Acadians were the Mi'Kmaq. It was not unexpected that the free-spirited Acadians ignored the British order of deportation. The insurgents were crudely armed and stood little chance to defeat the mighty British forces. Yet resist they did, even when it appeared that victory was not possible.

Like his father, *Beausoleil* was known by the British as a dissident at a young age. When he was only 21 years old, he and Jacques Michel were warned by the Nova Scotia Council to avoid associating with "warring Indians" and militant French missionaries. Around 1740, the Broussards established the hamlet which bore the name Village-des-Beausoleil, a village made up of only one family, near Boundary Creek (now the Village of Salisburg) on the north bank of the Petitcoudiac River ten miles from present-day Moncton, New Brunswick. At the time of the Battle of Minas in early 1747, *Beausoleil* gave assistance to Nicolas-Antoine Coulon de Villiers' troops who were fighting the British.[22] As a result of those military activities, Governor William Shirley of Massachusetts declared *Beausoleil* and eleven other Acadians "outlaws" for having provisioned the French troops. A reward of fifty pounds sterling was offered by the British "for the capture of each of these persons."

The following is an overview of the events leading to the expulsion: after the Treaty of Utrecht ceded Acadia to England in 1713, Acadians were commonly referred to as "French neutrals" by the British. Until 1755, Acadians were persistently threatened with deportation for their failure to take an unqualified oath to the British crown. They would only agree to a qualified oath that exempted them from taking up arms in case of conflict with the French. Simultaneously, they were under pressure from the French at Fort Louisbourg to take an unqualified oath of allegiance to the French king. As a result, Acadians lived in constant threat of expulsion from the British and retribution from French militants, such as the French Priest Abbé Jean-Louis LeLoutre.[23]

Tensions between France and England intensified in 1755, and Lieutenant Governor Charles Lawrence of Nova Scotia set up a trap for the Acadians. In July, 1755, a delegation of deputies from the Acadian community arrived at Halifax to make a presentation to the Governor's Council. They brought petitions that explained the Acadian position against signing an unqualified oath, and gave assurances that they would remain true to their conditional oath and remain neutral in any upcoming conflict. Their efforts failed because Lawrence had already made up his mind to deport the Acadians regardless of their position. The Acadian delegation was confined to the George's Island prison sheds in Halifax. The Acadian deputies now realized that the long standing threat of deportation was about to become a reality. By the end of August, there were as many as seventy deputies and priests in British custody awaiting their fate for the next two months. An order was issued: Acadians who were found anywhere in the province were to be taken into custody - even those who had taken unconditional oaths.

In 1755, Colonel John Winslow was the British officer in charge of the deportation in Grand Pré, the largest and most prosperous Acadian settlement in Acadie. In October of that year, he wrote a letter about the events of the dispersion to a friend in Boston.[24] The letter describes the confinement of about 1,500 Acadians at Grand Pré, "with no uncommon disturbances," but also reports the death of two young Acadians who apparently resisted the British. According to Winslow's letter, his troops were beginning to burn Acadian homes to discourage their return.

Some historians and writers have attributed the following quote to Colonel John Winslow:

> We are now hatching the noble and great project of banishing the French Neutrals from this province; they have ever been our secret enemies and have encouraged the Indians to cut our throats. If we can accomplish this expulsion, it will have been one of the greatest deeds the English in America have achieved; for among other considerations, the part of the country which they occupy is one of the best soils in the world, and, in the event, we might place some good farmers on their homesteads.

The preceding statement – the announcement of the "Great and Noble scheme" – was published in the colonial press. It was then, and remains today, a classic statement of the definition of ethnic cleansing. It is a model of ethnic cleansing from the prospective of the perpetrator. According to Yale history professor, Dr. John Mack Faragher, Director, Howard R. Lamar Center for the Study of Frontiers and Borders, it was probably not written by Winslow because he expressed some regret in his journal entries about the military operation that he was under orders to carry out. Dr. Faragher opines that the statement was more likely written by some member of the Governor's Council with close ties to Boston, where the report was first published.

In September, 1755, Winslow called together all of the Acadian males of the Grand Pré region over ten years of age. They were locked inside the church and told, "Your lands and tenements, cattle of all kinds and livestock of all sorts are forfeited to the Crown with all your other effects saving your money and household goods and you yourselves (will) be removed from this ... Province." [25] The transport ships arrived on August 30, 1755, at Grand Pré, and, on September 10, Winslow began loading the Acadian men aboard. The remainder of the transports did not arrive until October, at which time the families were boarded. He wrote the following in his journal: "The inhabitants, sadly and with great sorrow, abandoned their homes. The women, in great distress, carried their newborn or their youngest children in their arms. Others pulled carts with their household effects and crippled parents. It was a scene of confusion, despair, and desolation."

Beausoleil's role in leading the insurgency by Acadian militants is legendary. A detailed portrayal follows: Although the French army maintained a presence in Quebec and Fort Louisbourg (on Cape Breton Island), they were able to afford little assistance to those Acadians who resisted deportation. Led by the Broussard brothers, these resistance fighters met with some successes, to-wit: "During hard times over which they had little control, they defended what they felt they should defend, sometimes with caution like a fox, sometimes openly like *Beausoleil* Broussard or those unknown Acadians who defeated British soldiers in war at Bridgetown in 1757, in the famed Battle of Bloody Creek." [26] The body of water in Nova Scotia known as "Bloody Creek" got its name as a result of the English blood that flowed following a surprise attack by insurgents.

In June, 1755, the British, who were disputing possession of the Chignecto isthmus with the French, laid siege to Fort Beauséjour (near Sackville, New Brunswick). *Beausoleil* engaged in skirmishes against the British and in one outing, captured a British officer. In relating this incident, the French officer Louis-Thomas Jacau de Fiedmont testified that *Beausoleil* was recognized to be one of the bravest and most enterprising of the Acadians:

> The British captured one prisoner in this skirmish. On this same day the Acadian, Brossard, (also known as *Beausoleil*) and his band of Inhabitants were outside the French fort harassing the British, when they captured Ensign Hay of Hopson's Regiment. Ensign Hay was returning to the Camp at Butte à Mirande after visiting his wife at Fort Lawrence. A flag of truce from Beauséjour informed the British camp of his capture and that he was well." [27]

On June 16, 1755, the very day Fort Beauséjour capitulated, *Beausoleil* was so bold as to attack the British camp with sixty men, French and Mi'Kmaq. He lost only one man. Provided with safe conduct, he went to see Colonel Robert Monckton two days later to propose his acting as mediator between the British and the native peoples (Mi'Kmaq and Maliscets) in exchange for amnesty. Monckton agreed to this arrangement, subject, however, to the later approval of Lieutenant Governor Charles Lawrence. The following quote describes what occurred:

> Joseph Brossard, called *Beausoleil,* arrived under a safe-conduct to negotiate a peace with the Indians if the General would grant him an amnesty. M. Monckton received him kindly and pardoned him, but conditionally, subject to the approval of the Government. Jacob Maurice and a few settlers from Baye Verte also came with proposals. [28]

Beausoleil, known as an excellent marksman, was acknowledged by the British as being the leader of the resistance. According to one account, his resistance was so effective that British troops at Fort Cumberland were at times afraid to leave its walls. The following account describes the guerilla campaign around Fort Cumberland:

> The expulsion of the Acadians from Nova Scotia did not bring peace and safety to the Isthmus of Chignecto. The Acadians who had eluded capture continued, with their Indian allies, to harass the British on all possible occasions. Some were led by Brossard (*Beausoleil*), but most followed Charles de Champs de Boishébert. They lurked around the forts of the Isthmus, killing any soldiers who strayed beyond the safety of the posts and they were always ready to attack foraging parties. The guerilla bands moved swiftly from one place to another, keeping the British in a state of uncertainty as to when and where the next attack would occur. Boishébert was adept at evading British capture. Sometimes, when they reached a spot where he was reported to be, they would find the campfire ashes still warm but their quarry gone.[29]

The following British account by McCreath and Leefe shows how *Beausoleil* was able to terrorize the British by using brutal guerilla tactics, such as scalping the enemy:

> The spring of 1754 found yet another movement to establish new settlement, this one some ten miles east of Dartmouth. Twenty thousand acres were granted to twenty applicants who promised faithfully to provide twenty settlers for the proposed community which was suitably dubbed Lawrencetown. In May the settlers were sent there under the protective cover of two hundred regulars and rangers. Despite the early appearance of a blockhouse and picketed perimeter, the struggling settlement soon fell upon evil days. In an attack by Indians, four settlers and three soldiers were scalped. The raiders were led by Joseph Broussard, an Acadian who was perhaps better known by the pseudonym `Beausoleil.' An indefatigable foe of the British ...[30].

Obviously frustrated by the obstinate resistance, in one of his many dispatches to London, Lieutenant Governor Charles Lawrence suggested that the Acadian matter be resolved thusly:

I should think it would be of great advantage, both to them and us, that this matter was, one way or other, cleared up to them as soon as possible, because when they were sure of the situation they were to remain in, it would naturally produce a spirit of improvement amongst them, the advantages which they would soon be sensible of, and thereby become more attached to an English Government than they have hitherto been.[31]

Broussard matched his success on land with raids on coastal shipping.[32] He led a group of privateers, later referred to in the *Memoir on the Acadians* in *Archives Nationales* in Paris. [33]

After the decision was made to deport all Acadians, the British, in a preemptive strike, confined the more "war-like" Acadian men in Fort Lawrence. Most Acadians, however managed to abscond from the fort. The manner of evasion obviously helped to enhance *Beausoleil's* reputation as an innovative Acadian patriot: in the predawn hours of October 1, 1755, under the cover of a fierce thunderstorm, *Beausoleil* and a group of eighty-six Acadian insurgents imprisoned by the British in Fort Lawrence managed a daring breakout by digging a tunnel beneath the prison wall.[34] They quickly gathered their families, fled to the wilderness and aggressively fought the British until 1759. Yale historian Dr. John Mack Faragher, the Arthur Unobskey Professor of American History, describes the creative escape in his forthcoming book, *A Great and Noble Scheme: The Expulsion of the French Canadians:*

Using spoons, knives, and other tools smuggled in by their wives and mothers, who were supplying them with food and clothing, they dug a tunnel under the fort's walls. According to Acadian tradition, the men went out in order of size, from smallest to largest, each successive escapee squeezing through the passage and enlarging it for the next man. Last out was said to be René Richard *dit Le Petit René* — "Little René," the largest of all the prisoners. The escapees — including Joseph Broussard *dit Beausoleil* and several of his grown sons and nephews, but neither his son Victor nor his brother Alexandre, who remained imprisoned in Fort Cumberland — immediately joined forces with the Acadian resistance.[35]

Alexandre Broussard had been confined by the British at Fort Cumberland along with other Acadian insurgents.[36] Following *Beausoleil's* daring escape, the British became so alarmed that they imprisoned Alexandre and twenty-one others on the gunboat "Syren" under tighter security. On November 15, 1755, the gunboat escorted four shiploads of Acadian exiles from the Bay of Fundy to Charleston, South Carolina. Their ultimate destination was to have been the far southern colonies of South Carolina and Georgia, Lawrence having ordered that these militant Acadians from Chignecto "be removed to the greatest distance." Moreover, Alexandre and his fellow impounded insurgents were held in shackles on Sullivan's Island and labeled "special prisoners." *Beausoleil's* son, Victor-Gregoire, was among the prisoners. The wily Alexandre, even while under constant surveillance by the British in Charleston, still managed to flee from his captors. The local paper, the *South Carolina Gazette* reported the escape and referred to Alexandre as a "general of the Indians who escaped from a swamp and crossed the river at Maxwell's Bluff on a bark log." He and his group of four escapees, including Michel and Pierre Bastarache, obtained provisions by entering an absent planter's house and took what they needed for their trek back to Acadia. They made their way on foot back to what is now New Brunswick, where they rejoined *Beausoleil* and his loyalists, using Chipoudie as the base of the insurgency.

The remaining "special prisoners" at Charleston were summarily sent to London. The Acadians effectively used guerrilla warfare to fight the British, and thus they were considered to be some of the first Europeans to use such methods in North America.[37] After their escape, *Beausoleil* and his compatriots, Jean Basque and Simon Martin, led several successful attacks against the British.

Although *Beausoleil* assumed leadership for the Acadian militia, Alexandre was considered his equal. They had seven sons who were their clan lieutenants. There was an entire clan of Broussard insurgents in the lands west of Chipoudie Bay. Some stories tend to suggest that Alexandre was the dominant leader; legend seems to link all of the Broussards exploits into a composite embodiment called simply *Beausoleil.* One thing is certain: the resistance was very costly for the Broussard brothers. They suffered greatly and each lost his eldest son during the struggle. *Beausoleil* also lost his mother, wife and most of his children. In November, 1755, led by Major George Scott, the British

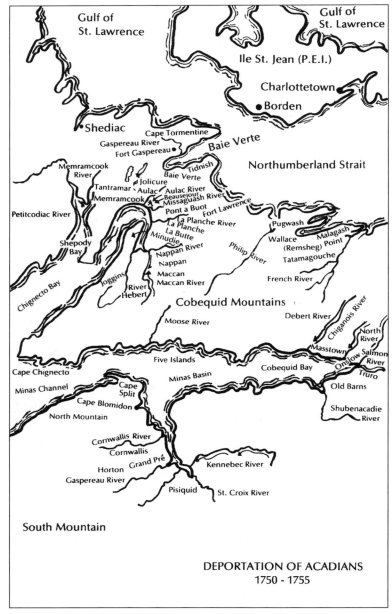

Source: Geoffrey Plank, *An Unsettled Conquest* (University of Pennsylvania Press, Philadelphia, Pennsylvania, 2001).

destroyed the Broussard's hamlet, Beausoleil Village.

The following shows the extreme precautions followed by the British patrols in order to avoid being discovered by the insurgents:

> While pleasures were occasional, warfare and danger were constant. In February of 1756, reports reached Colonel Scott that Boishébert and his band were at Shediac. Colonel Scott led a detachment there, hoping to attack the band – even, perhaps, to capture Boishébert himself. When the troops reached Shediac, they could find neither the leader nor his band. The British started their return to Fort Cumberland, only to be waylaid and attacked by Boishébert and his men. In the struggle, two soldiers were killed. Not long after this event, Boishébert sent a company of his Indians and Acadians to Baie Verte. There they burned a 100-ton schooner on the stocks and another at anchor nearby. During this action they killed seven British and took one prisoner. Searching parties suffered from the severe cold. *They were afraid to light camp fires lest the Indians and Acadians should spot them and many had their feet frozen.*[38]

Beausoleil commanded a privateer which operated in the Bay of Fundy and on the Petitcoudiac River. Aided by his four sons and the Acadian militia who had taken refuge along the Petitcoudiac River, he held [French] letters of marque from Governor Vaudreuil of New France,[39] and he continued to harass the British forces. In a letter to Amherst, the Commander at Halifax wrote:

> Captain Mackenzie (Commander at Fort Cumberland) acquaints me that he has received certain information that such of the Acadians as do not Surrender themselves intend to steal some of our Settlers Cattle for their Winters Subsistance [*sic*], in which they will be greatly assisted by the Vessels they are possessed of from the Indulgence of the Commander of His Majesty's Ships sent up this Year to the Bay of Chaleur, who it seems has given them passes to go all along the Coast wherever they please, which I suppose must have been obtained under pretence [*sic*] of their Surrendering themselves to some of His Majesty's Garrisons .... These people are Spirited up in their obstinacy by one *Beausoleil*

an Acadian, and two or three others who have already rendered themselves obnoxious to the English that they are conscious of the treatment they deserve at our hands, and therefore Stand out; if Captain MacKenzies parties are so lucky as to fall in with them the rest would soon surrender.[40]

It was probably during one of these encounters with the troops, commanded by George Scott, that *Beausoleil* was wounded. In November, 1758, Scott led British troops to "lay waste" the Petitcoudiac region. The British burned all of the Acadian hamlets. In response to a bounty by the government, many Acadians, including women and children, were killed and actually scalped. A battle ensued, and *Beausoleil* suffered a serious wound to his foot and was obliged to go to the other side of the Miramichi River for recuperation. The following palpably shows the brutality of the means utilized by the insurgency:

Danks and seventy-five of the men landed and hid in the woods, while the sloop sailed up the river to decoy the enemy. About noon, thirty of the enemy proceeded to fire the vessel. Danks and his men then rushed from the woods and surrounded them. The British killed and scalped three men, took nine prisoners and drove fourteen into the river. Danks, reputed to be a brutal man, led his men in shooting at the Acadians and Indians who had chosen to brave the swirling, muddy waters rather than submit to capture. Ten of them drowned or were shot, the rest escaped. The next day, Danks sailed up the river in his sloop, and the Acadians fired on him from both sides of the river. A party of Danks' men landed, marched to a village and burned it, taking away furniture and livestock. They searched the banks of the river without finding anything, and returned to Ford Cumberland without suffering any casualties.[41]

It is believed that the British repeatedly attempted to kill or capture *Beausoleil,* but were unable to do so. British Captain Mackenzie wrote to Colonel Forster:

Such of the above Acadians as I was informed had been privateering or pirating Since they Sent in their deputies to Submit to Colonel Frye are confined according to your orders, One or two of these deputies and all the other principals that remain'd [*sic*] are in this number; So that there remains now on the Coast only one of any note among them (*BeauSoleil*) who lived at a distance from the rest and retired thirty leagues into the Woods upon having Intelligence of us; This fellow I believe may be Catch'd [sic] this Winter or Spring by a Scout upon Snow Shoes which I will be ready to try if you think him worth So much notice.[42]

In July, 1758, Fort Louisbourg was captured by the British, so the militant partisans' ability to acquire arms and supplies ended. Due to the dire circumstances in which the Acadian insurgents found themselves, they realized that all hope for victory was lost. Many of the captives died from exposure and starvation. The gravity of the situation can be seen clearly with an appreciating of the harshness of the winters in Acadie:

> By the latter part of March, provisions became scarce, and men and officers alike were on short allowances. By March 29th, a sloop which had been frozen in the Basin all winter managed to make her way through the ice to go to Boston for supplies. By April, flocks of wild fowl had returned to their nesting grounds on the marshes, providing a supply of fresh meat. Spring also brought small numbers of Indians and Acadians around the fort.[43]

In October, 1759, General Edward Whitmore, the British governor at Louisbourg, issued a proclamation offering the Acadian insurgents an "olive branch." Jacques Manach, a missionary priest, was enlisted by the Acadians to mediate. On November 16, 1759, after the fall of Quebec, and in obvious response to the British offer of amnesty, *Beausoleil* and Alexandre proceeded to Fort Cumberland (Fort Beauséjour) to present a proposal for their surrender with the proviso that they would be allowed to remain in the province and practice their religion.[44] On behalf of the estimated two hundred Acadian partisans, a document was presented by *Beausoleil* to Major Fyre, the British commanding officer. Dr. John Mack Faragher believes that *Beausoleil* left Alexandre as a hostage and then returned to assemble the insurgents but foresaw that the British were setting a trap to deport everyone, so he did not surrender. *Beausoleil,* along with the few remaining insurgents, moved north to Boishébert's camp at Petit-Rochelle where they finally surrendered to British expeditionary forces in July, 1760, at the mouth of the Restigouche River. A second group of 700 freedom fighters led by resistance fighter Pierre II Surette, and his friends, Jean and Michel Bourque, also surrendered:

> In November of 1759, four deputies, Alexander Brussard, Simon Martin, Jean Bass and Joseph Brussard arrived at Fort Cumberland, acting as spokesmen for some 190 Acadians around Memramcook and Petitcodiac. They asked Colonel Frye, commander at Ford Cumberland, for food and shelter. Colonel Frye agreed to help them as much as possible and gave them permission to occupy abandoned buildings around the fort. Two days later, deputies representing some 700 Acadians from the Miramichi, Richibucto, and Buctouche areas, arrived at the Fort to tender their surrender and ask for help. As many as possible were allowed to come to Fort Cumberland.[45]

By 1760, nearly all of the Acadian insurgents (estimated to be 900) were imprisoned by the British at Fort Cumberland. According to Faragher, the offer of amnesty by the British was merely a ploy made in the name of the Crown because General Edward Whitmore wrote to Lawrence saying that despite the promise he made, he was in favor of sending the incendiaries to England. In compliance with those recommendations, the refugees were summarily marched to Halifax, where they were imprisoned behind the palisades of Georges Island.

Although most of the Acadia militia had been captured or surrendered to the British by 1760, *Beausoleil's* brother, Jean Baptiste Broussard, refused to surrender.[46] In October, 1759, having spent a fifth devastating winter in the forest, the Acadian insurgency was all but starved. Jean Baptiste swore he would never surrender. He and his family set out on foot and walked across all of what is now New Brunswick, Canada, in the dead of winter, reaching Quebec and French resistance fighters in May, 1760. His obstinacy caused his family tremendous suffering. Only one son and one daughter survived the trek. Along this trail lay the graves of his wife, two of his children, and his mother-in-law. True to his word, Jean Baptiste never surrendered and eventually returned to Quebec, bringing his surviving son and daughter with him.

What motivated *Beausoleil* and his brothers to resist so fiercely? To find the answer one would need to examine his effort toward self-definition: his occupation, activities, personal traits, relationship to the environment and leisure activities, but because so little is known about him, we can only surmise. Everyone seemed to agree on one trait: he was a determined man, known as having a fixed purpose with a firm and unwavering resolve to save his Acadian culture. He, like the British of this era, engaged in brutal activities which caused retribution and resulted in his family experiencing much suffering. He is credited with leading these European descendants in their use of guerrilla tactics. The crudely armed Acadians learned these tactics from the Mi'Kmaq and they were often successful. During the resistence *Beausoleil* often engaged in battles aided by Mi'Kmaq. It is believed that he also learned many values from the Mi'Kmaq, such as personal honor.

Obviously, *Beausoleil's* suspicion of the sincerity of General Edward Whitmore's offer of amnesty was proven correct by the British's actions. *Beausoleil* appeared to the British to have a sixth sense. He earned the respect and fear of the British by his uncanny ability to anticipate and understand their motives. The British feared *Beausoleil* because he showed by his actions that he was determined to do what was necessary in order to resist the Acadian assimilation into the hated British civilization.

CHAPTER 5
FINALIZING THE ACADIAN PROBLEM

Following the French and Indian War, the "Acadian problem" facing British authorities seemed insurmountable: Acadia, once a province in colonial Canada, no longer existed outside of historical memory. Yet, the Acadians considered themselves neither French nor British subjects. Over the years, the Acadians had developed a distinctive ethnic identity as they continued to resist assimilation into British society.

Charles Lawrence, the architect of the Acadian deportation, died in Halifax in October, 1760, and was buried beneath St. Paul's Church. Obviously, he was despised by the Acadians; surprisingly, he was likewise disdained by his own contemporaries. In 1757, he was described by his subordinates as having a "wicked mind" and an "oppressive and tyrannical personality."

Lawrence was replaced by Governor Jonathan Belcher, a member of the Nova Scotian Council that had issued the order of expulsion. Belcher had written a memorandum "justifying" the deportation under British law. Belcher feared for his life. He suspected that the Acadian prisoners at Halifax plotted to escape and murder him. As a result, he sought to have *Beausoleil* and the militant Acadians deported. Despite his request to the Lords of Trade seeking authorization to do so, they strongly advised him to allow the remaining Acadians to stay in the province.

With the fall of St. Johns (Newfoundland) to the French forces in June, 1762, Belcher again feared a bloody uprising by the Acadians. He consulted General Amherst to obtain permission to deport the prisoners. The Lords of Trade in London were not consulted. With only General Amherst's approval, the Nova Scotia Council declared martial law on July 13 and sent the militia across the province to gather up as many of the remaining Acadians as possible and to march them to Halifax.[47] Apparently fearing *Beausoleil*'s presence in the Halifax prison, he and his son, Joseph, and Anselme, the son of Alexandre, were brought and held at Fort Edward in Windsor, Nova Scotia, a considerable distance from Halifax. Other members of the Broussard family remained on Georges Island. Clearly, for security reasons, Governor Belcher felt it wise not to allow the Broussard clan to remain together – even in confinement.

By July, 1762, the situation had worsened. Some Acadians had threatened to "cut the throats" of the landowners who occupied former Acadians' lands. Although there is no historical evidence to support this fact, the British in Halifax believed that *Beausoleil* had led an attack in 1751 on the village of Dartmouth, located near Halifax. Therefore, those Acadians at large were then returned and placed in Georges Island prison camp.

Belcher was determined to rid the province of the "Acadian problem" once and for all. In August, 1762, over 1,200 prisoners had been placed aboard ships which sailed to Boston. However, the Massachusetts Council, weary of the problems and expense of caring for refugees from Nova Scotia, refused to accept them and they were returned to Halifax. Due to the inability of Governor Belcher to properly administer the "Acadian problem" and other criticisms of his administration, he was replaced by Montague Wilmot. The Board of Trade had come to the conclusion that the expulsions should end, but Wilmot did not agree with this position. Although he had no intention of releasing the enemy combatants despite the orders that they should remain in the province, Wilmot grudgingly acknowledged that these prisoners had rights.

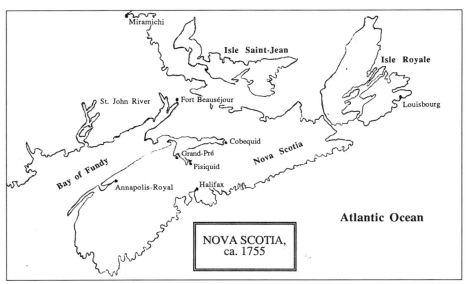

In the spring of 1763, *Beausoleil* was still confined at Fort Edwards. The British discovered that he was in possession of a letter written by the Ambassador of France in which the Acadians were urged to leave and return to France. It is believed that *Beausoleil* intended to deliver this missive to an Acadian loyalist named Joseph Le Maigre. This proved quite alarming to Wilmot, who viewed it as proof that regardless of the location of *Beausoleil* within the province, he continued to present a clear and present danger to peace, as well as a serious threat of renewed insurrection by the Acadian partisans. *Beausoleil* was forthwith returned to Georges Island prison where he remained under the highest level of security. As a result of the arrival of 900 Acadian insurgents, security on Georges Island prison was drastically increased, especially because one of the prisoners was *Beausoleil*, the most feared of all the partisans.[48]

Life for the Acadian prisoners behind the island's palisades was extremely difficult. Their warm clothing had been taken from them and many became ill from exposure and malnutrition. With the exception of the leaders of the resistance movement, the prisoners were either deported or put to work on farms which had once been owned by these same Acadians. The settlers which the British had brought in to take over the Acadian farms were unfamiliar with the complex system of dikes. Therefore, they requested that the government allow the Acadian prisoners to help rebuild the systems that had fallen into decay and disrepair during the war. As a result of these requests, the government allowed the Acadians to earn a wage which was used to supplement their meager rations, thereby making them strong enough for the heavy manual labor demanded of them.

For *Beausoleil* and his partisans however, the situation was much different. Broussard, Surette and the Bourque brothers, along with their family members and supporters, were not permitted this limited freedom from confinement. Government officials were fearful that they presented a compelling threat to British officials due to their desire to exact revenge. Accordingly, *Beausoleil* and his group of loyalists remained in confinement on Georges Island.

Despite the inhospitable conditions, some Acadians were able to carry on a semblance of normalcy through marriages. Protestant clergymen performed these rituals for them because there were no Catholic priests available to do so. Later, upon arrival in Louisiana, many of the Acadian couples renewed their marriage vows and had their children baptized by

Catholic priests. In 1763, Elizabeth Isabelle Broussard, granddaughter of *Beausoleil*, was born in the island prison camp, where many families had been detained. However, Joseph Gregoire Broussard, the eldest son of Alexandre, died, leaving his widow, Ursule Trahan, and their three children under the protection of his father.

Henri-Dominique Parette summarized the situation:

> Acadian militias were not used by the French as much as they could have been against British authorities, who considered Acadians to be prisoners of war even in peacetime. History cannot be rewritten and it would be silly to fight on paper the battles of the past. It is important, though, to view Acadians as an intelligent and well-organized community and not as passive peasants waiting to be expelled. Such a view provides Acadians of today, and all of us, with a better idea of who those pioneers really were. They were not cowards, nor were they traitors. During hard times over which they had little control, they defended what they felt they should defend, sometimes with caution like a fox, sometimes openly like *Beausoleil* Broussard.[49]

The brutal imprisonment of *Beausoleil* was often referred to by historians as simply a period of "detainment." Now, thanks to the excellent research by Dianne Marshall, we know the truth: British fear of Acadian retaliation caused much suffering to the estimated 1,000 Acadians who remained in Nova Scotia in 1764. The man most responsible for British paranoia was arguably *Beausoleil*. Ironically, his tactics, which had served him so well, and his determination to defend his homeland, ultimately changed the image of Acadians and linked his descendants forever to his beloved Acadia.

CHAPTER 6
DEPARTING FOR A NEW LIFE

The Acadians had always been deft negotiators with the British. It is not known how the remaining Acadians schemed to obtain British permission allowing them to depart from Nova Scotia in 1764. There is scant firsthand evidence on the details. Certainly their reputation as militants who resisted accepting unnecessary authority presented a great challenge to Governor Wilmot, who devised a proposal which would prove unacceptable to the Acadians. Even in the face of known dangers, the Acadians decided to depart for a new life rather than succumb to British demands.

In 1763, the Treaty of Paris was signed, ending the French and Indian War. At the end of the hostilities, based upon a list of Acadians waiting to go to a French territory, there were approximately 1,019 Acadians in Nova Scotia.[50] This information was contained in a letter written by *Beausoleil* and presented to the Council at Halifax on August 18, 1763. In 1764, Wilmot again attempted to finalize the "Acadian problem." He proposed that the remaining prisoners be sent to the French West Indies. He strenuously argued that, even though Britain was no longer at war with France, to allow the Acadians to resettle in the province would be too dangerous for the British inhabitants. However, the British Board of Trade in London was not convinced to change their policy. Lord Halifax, head of the British Board of Trade, again directed Wilmot to allow the Acadians to remain in Nova Scotia "consistent with public peace and security" which, of necessity, required the obligatory oath of allegiance to the King of England.

In order to circumvent the clear directive of the Board of Trade, Wilmot, along with the Council, promulgated a devious scheme by setting forth the following order which was intended to dissuade Acadians from remaining within the province. They would be settled in groups of no more than ten, at great distances from one another and would be required to sign an oath that was anti-Catholic. Understandably, the Acadians had tired of the suffering and struggle. Some reluctantly agreed to the conditions while many others chose to depart the province for Quebec. However, for security reasons, Quebec was not allowed as an option for *Beausoleil* and his followers because the British felt that he would have been still too close geographically to Nova Scotia and would be able to exact revenge and foment rebellion.

The partisans decided that their only hope to preserve their culture and avoid assimilation into British society was to leave the province. Therefore, using funds that had been amassed from Acadian labors on the dikes and by selling whatever possessions they still owned, the prisoners arranged to hire ships to take them to Saint-Domingue (Haiti) in the French West Indies.

Led by *Beausoleil*, two groups of more than six hundred Acadians left Halifax for the French West Indies in December, 1764, and in the spring of 1765. The group included most of *Beausoleil's* and Alexandre's living relatives. Due to disease and unbearable heat, many Acadians died once they arrived in Saint-Domingue. It is believed that Agnès Thibodeau Broussard, *Beausoleil's* wife, died on the island. The departure is thus described by Dr. Carl A. Brasseaux:

> Free to execute their designs, approximately six hundred Acadians, led by Joseph Broussard *dit Beausoleil*, chartered 'Vessels at their own Expense' and, in late November or early December, 1764, began the first segment of their roundabout voyage to Illinois. Unable to complete their preparations before the onset of winter, however, numerous other Acadians, 'amounting to as many more, in different parts of the Province,' made ready to depart for 'the same destination' in the early spring of 1765.[51]

On February 28, 1765, *Beausoleil's* group of 193 Acadians arrived in New Orleans. The former French colony of Louisiana had been secretly ceded to Spain. When word reached the French government headed by Commissioner Nicolas Foucault, he was alarmed that such a large number of Acadians had arrived in the struggling colony. Nevertheless, *Beausoleil* was received as a French hero. The French colonial officials wrote a "Report on the Paper Money Held by the Acadians." In the report, the French officials acknowledged *Beausoleil* as the leader of the first Acadians from Halifax to arrive, viz:

To wit, From one Broussard, [*Beausoleil*] leader of the first group [of Acadians] to reach this colony, composed of 58 families, the sum of 33,395 *livres,* 18 *sols,* divided unequally among the 58 families. The ledger for said amount has been sent to France as supporting evidence, attached to the papers which it represents.[52]

Initially, officials wanted to settle the refugees on the right bank of the Mississippi River near New Orleans. However, the proposed settlement site flooded frequently and would have required considerable work because it was covered by a dense hardwood forest. Some of the Acadians went to join exiles who had settled upriver at St. James parish. Negotiations followed for about two months and most of the Acadians, including Alexandre and *Beausoleil,* were authorized to migrate to the Poste des Attakapas near present day St. Martinville in southwest Louisiana.

Brasseaux opined that *Beausoleil's* ultimate plans were to ascend the Mississippi River and settle in the Illinois area. However, due to the receptiveness shown by the officials in New Orleans, the group accepted an offer to settle lands in Louisiana. He explains:

Such expectations were entertained most faithfully by the displaced former members of the Acadian resistance. Led by Joseph Broussard *dit Beausoleil,* 193 Acadians departed the Nova Scotian capital in late November, changed ship at Saint-Domingue, and arrived at New Orleans in late February, 1765. The immigrants' impoverishment elicited genuine compassion among Louisiana's leading officials. Although Choiseul, the French minister of marine, had authorized only essential expenditures by the caretaker government, Commissaire-ordonnateur Denis-Nicolas Foucault, chief administrative officer, provided the immigrants, whose number by April, 1765, would grow to 231, with foodstuffs, tools, muskets, and building materials worth 15,500 livres.[53]

Brasseaux estimates that when the Acadian deportation commenced in 1755, there were approximately 15,000 Acadians in Acadie.[54] An estimated one-third of these Acadians died or were killed by the British. One-third migrated to other parts of the world and one-third escaped deportation or returned to live in Nova Scotia and New Brunswick. The British effort of ethnic cleansing was one of the first attempted in North America. Due to the heroic efforts of *Beausoleil*, his trusted lieutenant Alexandre and his Acadian militia, and other insurgents, those efforts failed and the Acadian culture survived.[55] Brasseaux describes the Halifax-Acadian migration to Louisiana:

> The exodus of hundreds of Acadian 'survivors' from post expulsion Nova Scotia signaled not the final chapter for a frontier-spawned culture, but the beginning of a major experiment in cultural transplantation. Unwilling to abandon their ethnic identity for the privilege of becoming proper British Protestants and for continued servitude to the oppressive colonial regime, most, though not all, of the Acadians captured in the Seven Years' War preferred to carve out a new life in an alien land rather than to face the insidious death of assimilation. Undeterred by the challenge, the *émigrés* readily faced the task of rebuilding their lives and reuniting their large extended families in a stable, francophone environment.[56]

Each successive generation added its own touch to the telling and retelling of the Acadians' plight, but the core story of the exodus remained intact: they were overall, an oppressed people and not blood-thirsty buccaneers, as perceived by British officials. In the end, Wilmot's concocted plan to rid the province of *Beausoleil* and the insurgents was successful. Ironically, it ensured the continuation of the Acadian culture in Louisiana which was called Acadie du sud (Acadia of the south) by the Acadians.

54

REPORT ON PAPER MONEY HELD BY ACADIANS

New Orleans, March 8, 1766

AGI, Audiencia de Santo Domingo, 2585:non-paginated

Register of sums, as much from letters of exchange, card money, and drafts, as certificates and other negotiable bills, formerly used as specie by the Acadian refugees in this colony. They have delivered these papers to Mister Maxent, for shipment to his correspondent in France, whom he will instruct to seek reimbursement [from the French government], March 8, 1766.

To wit,

From one Broussard,[88] leader of the first group [of Acadians] to reach this colony, composed of 58 families, the sum of 33,395 *livres*, 18 *sols*, divided unequally among the said 58 families. The ledger for said amount has been sent to France as supporting evidence, attached to the papers which it represents.— 33,395#18^s

From one Bergeron,[89] the sum of 47,076 *livres* [pounds], 19 *sols* [schillings], 6 *deniers* [pence], belonging to 73 families, some of whom arrived in June 1765, and the remainder of whom will arrive at the first opportunity.—47,076#19^{s}6^d

From one Lachausée,[90] 27,044 *livres*, 7 *sols*, 8 *deniers*, belonging to 37 families, some of whom reached this colony in various ships—in August, September, October and November—and the remainder will arrive shortly.—27,044#7^{s}8^d

[This ledger] does not include several certificates whose value has not yet been determined, and, [consequently, they] were not included in the total of the foregoing ledgers. I hereby acknowledge receipt of the aforementioned sums, in the aforementioned currency, for the aforementioned purposes.
At New Orleans   (signed) Maxent

Total—107,517#5^{s}2^d

[88]Joseph Broussard *dit* Beausoleil.

[89]Probably Jean-Baptiste Bergeron, a resident of the Cabannocé post (present-day St. James Parish). Voorhies, *Louisianians*, p. 116.

[90]Philippe Lachausée, a French physician married to an Acadian. *Ibid.*, pp. 424- 425.

Source: Carl Brasseaux, *Quest for the Promised Land* (U.S.L. Center for Louisiana Studies, 1989).

CHAPTER 7
THE SETTLEMENT OF "NEW ACADIA"

The establishment of "New Acadia" in southwestern Louisiana set the stage for the development of the Cajun culture. In the 1990 U.S. census, 668,000 people claimed descendancy from Acadians. Cajun ethnicity remains positive and strong. Why does Cajun culture endure? The answer involves both social and historical analysis of the original *émigrés*. Today, *Beausoleil* remains the symbolic leader and there are, understandably, attempts to reconstruct his life in literature, music, art, archeology and family reunions. This movement ensures continuation of "New Acadia."

Beausoleil and other Acadian leaders needed to develop a means of survival in their new adopted homeland. The Treaty of Paris had ceded French lands east of the Mississippi River to Great Britain. Previously, these lands supplied meat for New Orleans. The Acadians had raised cattle in Chipoudie, and *Beausoleil*, learning that New Orleans needed a new source of meat to supply the growing population, entered into negotiations with Frenchmen Sieur Antoine Bernard Dauterive and André Masse. On March 3, 1765, the Frenchmen agreed to relinquish their titles to lands in the Attakapas, resulting in a contract dated April 4, 1765, with retired French army captain Sieur Antoine Bernard Dauterive. The contract, by which all parties mortgaged all of their property, provided the Acadians with cattle for breeding purposes. The Acadians were each to receive some land, along with five cows (and their calves) and one bull for six successive years. As a form of "sharecropping," after six years, they were required to return the initial investment and half of the offspring in repayment of their contract.

Acadians who were bound by the document, called the Dauterive Compact (see document on page 51), were *Beausoleil*, Pierre Arceneaud, Alexandre Broussard, Jean-Baptiste Broussard, Victor Broussard, Jean Duga, Joseph Guillbeau and Oliver Thibaudau.[57] Interestingly, the document recited that "the Acadians having declared that they did not know how to sign." This contract was the origination of the Acadian cattle industry in Louisiana. Parties to the contract were Victor Broussard, one of *Beausoleil's* sons, and Jean-Baptiste Broussard, the son of Alexandre. On April 30, 1765, the governor reported that 231

(58-60 families) Acadians had departed New Orleans for settlement in the Attakapas and Opelousas Districts. They had been provided with provisions, merchandise, and seventy-one grenadier muskets with ammunition. Eventually, the Acadians were driving cattle to New Orleans for sale, just like their ancestors had herded and steered cattle to Acadian posts on the Chignecto Bay.

According to local historians Donald Arceneaux and George Bentley, well before 1750 André Masse was trading with the Attakapas Indians. In 1763, Masse sent a request to French authorities for a grant of land to the west of the St. Martinville area from Bayou Tortue to Bayou Vermilion. In the petition, he stated that he had been operating a cattle ranch in the Attakapas since 1747. Masse, his slaves, and the free persons-of-color living with him, can be considered the first non-native settlers in the Attakapas District. Masse was a sponsor at the baptism of an Acadian infant in the Attakapas in 1765, and he later signed the baptismal record of another Acadian child as well. By 1765, Masse had entered into a partnership with Antoine Dauterive. The partners were given the same land Masse requested in 1763. Dauterive himself appears to have claimed the land along the Teche at St. Martinville to Bayou Tortue. Dauterive never permanently lived on his Attakapas land. He had another cattle operation and plantation on the Mississippi River across from Bayou Manchac. He maintained a "road," or more likely a trail, from the Mississippi River to the Atchafalaya River and then on to the Attakapas to bring his cattle to market in New Orleans.

The Acadians quickly prospered in their new homeland. By the 1780s, the Broussard land holdings extended from St. Martinville to Bayou Vermilion. Two hundred thirty-five cattle brands were registered in the name of Broussard. Many direct descendants of *Beausoleil* continue the cattle business in Vermilion Parish.

The crowning achievement of *Beausoleil's* life occurred in Louisiana. The Spanish governor Charles Aubry issued a special commission on April 8, 1765, naming *Beausoleil* as "Captain of the Militia and Commandant of the Acadians of the Attakapas." [58] After many years of leading his people through great difficulties, he finally received the official recognition of something everyone accepted as fact: he was named leader or "Chief" of the Acadians in the Attakapas District. This would be as close as he would come during his lifetime to receiving redemption.

Joseph "Beausoleil" Broussard Named Captain Commandant

Below is a copy of page 189 from *Southwest Louisiana Biographical and Historical* edited by William Henry Perrin (The Gulf Publishing Company, 1891 and reprinted by Claitor's Publishing Division, Baton Rouge, 1971) which is a French (left) and English (right) reproduction of the Commission of Captain Commandant of the Acadian Militia issued on April 8, 1765 to Joseph "Beausoleil" Broussard by Charles Philipe Aubry, Spanish Governor of Louisiana.

COMMISSION DE CAPITAINE COMMAN-DANT DE MILICE POUR LE NOMME GAURHEPT BROUSSARD, DIT BEAU SOLEIL.

Charles Philipe Aubry, Chevalier de L'ordre Royale et Militaire de St. Louis, Commandant pour le Roy de la Province de la Louisiane.

Attendu les preuves de valeur, de fidélité et d'attachement pour le service du Roy que le nommé Gaurhept Broussard, dit Beau Soleil, Acadien, a donné dans différentes occasions, et les témoignages honorables que Mr. le Marquis de Vaudreuil, et autres gouverneurs-généraux du Canada luy ont accordé en consideration de ses blessures, et de son courage dont il a donné des preuves autentiques dans différentes affaires contre les ennemis de sa majesté. Nous l'établissons Capitaine de Milice et Commandant des Acadiens qui sont venu avec lui d'Angleterre et qui vont s'établir sur la terre des Acutapas, ne doutant point qu'il ne se comporte toujours avec le même zèle, et la même fidélité pour le service du Roy, et étant persuadé qu'il montrera toujours à ses compatriotes le bon exemple pour la sagesse, la vertu, la religion, et l'attachement pour son prince. Enjoignons aux susdits habitants Acadiens de luy obéir, et entendre à tout ce qu'il leurs commandera pour le service du Roy sous peine de désobéissance.

Mandons aux officiers des troupes entretenus en cette province de faire reconnaitre le dit Gaurhept Broussard, dit Beau Soleil, en la dite qualité de Capitaine Commandant des Acadiens qui vont s'établir aux Acutapas de tous ceux et ainsy qu'il appartiendra. En foy de quoy nous avons signé ces présentes et a celle fait opposer le sceau de nos armes et contresigné par notre secrétaire, à la Nouvelle-Orléans en notre hotel, le 8 avril, 1765.

[Signé] AUBRY. { Sceau }
Consignée par
  MONSEIGNEUR JOUKIE.
Copié par J. O. Broussard.

COMMISSION OF CAPTAIN COMMAND-ANT OF MILITIA FOR THE HERE NAMED GAURHEPT BROUSSARD SURNAMED BEAU SOLEIL.

Charles Philipe Aubry, Knight of the Royal and Military Order of St. Louis, Commandant for the King of the Province of Louisiana:

In view of the proofs of valor, fidelity and attachment in the service of the King which the herein named Gaurhept Broussard, surnamed Beau Soleil, Acadian, has given on different occasions, and of the honorable testimonials which the Marquis of Vaudreuil and other Governors General of Canada, have accorded him in consideration of his wounds and of the courage which he has given proof of in different affairs against the enemies of his Majesty. We appoint him Captain of Militia and Commandant of the Acadians, who have come with him from England to settle on the land of the Acutapas; having no doubt that he will always comport himself with the same zeal, and the same fidelity, in the service of the King; and being persuaded that he will always show his fellow countrymen a good example in wisdom, virtue and religion, and attachment for his Prince. We enjoin on the herein mentioned Acadian inhabitants to obey him, and lend an ear to all which he will command them in the service of the King, under penalty of disobedience.

We direct the officers of the troops kept in this Province to have the said Gaurhept Broussard, surnamed Beau Soleil, recognized in designated capacity of Captain Commandant of the Acadians, who are going to establish themselves among the Acutapas, and of all those as of right shall appertain. In faith of which we have signed these presents, and to them have affixed the seal of our arms, and our secretary has countersigned the same in New Orleans, at our hotel, April 8, 1765.

[Signed] AUBRY. { SEAL. }
Countersigned by
  MONSEIGNEUR JOUKIE.
Copied by J. O. Broussard.

Commandant Broussard was the progenitor of the Broussard family in Southwest Louisiana. He has left a large representation of descendants to perpetuate his name.

Note that *Beasoleil's* first name was incorrectly listed as "Gaurhept."

Attakapas District's treeless prairies consisted of the present-day St. Martin, Lafayette, Vermilion, Iberia and St. Mary parishes. The broad grasslands were easy to settle as herds of cattle roamed the countryside. Even though some Acadians had settled around St. James Parish earlier, interspersed with families of different European extraction, the *Beausoleil* Acadians were the first to settle in the Attakapas District and establish an identifiable cultural dominance in the region. Others had resisted settling there because of the supposed "man eating" Attakapas Indians who had long inhabited the area. Yet, because these Acadians had been closely aligned with the native people in Acadie, notably the Mi'Kmaq, they readily accepted the Spanish government's offer of land grants. The *Beausoleil* group was made up of extended families of the Broussard, Trahan, Thibodeaux and Guilbeaux clans that had migrated from the Petitcoudiac and Miramichi Rivers. Shortly after signing the Dauterive Compact, some of the Acadians moved to the Fausse Pointe area located along the eastern ridge of Bayou Teche.

Soon after their arrival in the Fausse Pointe area, a severe epidemic developed which probably caused the deaths of the Broussard brothers. From July through November, 1765, thirty-nine Acadian burial services were performed. Although it is unknown where they are buried, cousins Donald Arceneaux, a native of Lafayette, Louisiana, and George Bentley, a native of New Iberia, Louisiana, and descendants of both Broussard brothers, believe that their graves are located near Loreauville along the bayou banks on the east side of the Bayou Teche. The evidence indicates that *Beausoleil* is probably buried at the Fausse Pointe turn of the Bayou Teche, in the area of Loreauville, and they argue persuasively that Alexandre is probably buried in the Belle Place area (south of Loreauville) since it is known that in 1765 three of Alexandre's sons, and his son-in-law, Jean Trahan, were occupying that area and immediate family members of Alexandre, including his wife, are buried at "le dernier camp d'en bas" (the last camp below – at the end). Under the direction of Dr. Mark A. Rees, Professor of Anthropology at the University of Louisiana at Lafayette, an archaeology field school investigated the former location of the Amand Broussard house, which is now located at Vermilionville, a historical park in Lafayette, Louisiana. Artifacts from the original site include predominantly late eighteenth-century and early nineteenth-century ceramics. Further reconnaissance-level surveys are planned to locate areas likely to have been the campsites of the first generation of Acadians in the region (le camp d'en bas, la dernier camp d'en bas, Camp Beausoleil), as well as the burial place of *Beausoleil* and the other sixteen *émigrés* who died in the area in 1765, probably from an epidemic of yellow fever. Real-Time Thermal Imaging, a company based in Kenner, Louisiana, specializing in the location of old grave sites, has agreed to assist with the work. According to Dr. Rees, the first phase of the project has been completed.

There is some uncertainty surrounding the date of *Beausoleil*'s death: Church records from St. Martinville archives show that a Joseph Broussard died on September 4, 1765.[59] However, Jean-François de Cenrey Capuchin, a Franciscan missionary priest, performed the burial service for Joseph *dit Beausoleil* Broussard on October 20, 1765. The document was recorded on November 25, 1765. Coincidently, Alexandre died on September 18, 1765. A translation of the document found in the church archives reads:

> ... the year 1765, September 7th, I, Prêtre Capucin [Capuchine] Missionnaire Apostolique Curé of the Nouvelle Acadie, certify that the body of Marguerite Thibodeaux, wife of Alexandre Broussard, and Joseph Broussard, were buried on the 5th of this month, died the day before [September 4], ...[60]

Much of the information on *Beausoleil*'s death was compiled by Donald Joseph Arceneaux, who developed a comprehensive list of persons interred at various burial locations in the area from July 26 to November 2, 1765, in the Attakapas District of Spanish Louisiana. This is what Arceneaux believes:

> I believe that the 'Joseph Broussard' who died on September 4, 1765, and was buried on September 5 at 'le dernier camp d'en bas' is most probably a different Joseph Broussard from 'Joseph *dit Beausoleil* Broussard' who was buried on October 20 at Camp Beausoleil. Marguerite Broussard, wife of Alexandre, died in the epidemic and was also buried on September 5 at 'le denier camp d'en bas.' Father Francois recorded both of the September 5 burials on September 7, and recorded the burial of 'Joseph *dit Beausoleil* Broussard' on November 25. Why would Father Francois make two different registry dates, one in September

8

Sep. Joseph Belle Fontaine	))	Le deux Septembre le corps de feu Joseph Belle Fontaine a été inhumé en premier Camp d'en bas, en foy de quoy j'ay signé aux Atakapas les jours et an que dessus et est signé F. Jean Francois Curé.
Sep. Margueritte Thibodeaux epouse d'Alexandre Broussard, Sep. Joseph Broussard	))))))	L'an mil sept cent soixante cinq, le sept Septembre je, pretre Capucin Missionaire Apostolique Curé de la Nlle [Nouvelle] Acadie soussigné certifie que les corps de Margueritte Thibodeaux épouse vivante d'Alexandre Broussard, et celui de Joseph Broussard ont été inhumés le cinq du présent, décèdés la veille, au dernier Camp d'en bas, en foy de quoy j'ay signé les jours et an que dessus et est, signé F. Jean Francois Curé qui signa.
Sep. Alexandre Broussard	))	L'an mil sept cent soixante cinq, le vingt-deux Septembre, je, pretre Capucin Missionaire Apostolique Curé de la Nlle [Nouvelle] Acadie soussigné certifie que le dix huit du courant le corps de feu Alexandre Broussard a été inhumé au Camp d'en bas, en foy de quoy j'ay signé aux Atakapas.
Sep. Jean Dugas et Francois Arsenaud ou Arsenaux	))))	L'an mil sept cent soixante cinq, le vingt-deux septembre, je pretre Capucin Missionaire Apostolique, Curé de la Nlle [Nouvelle] Acadie soussigné certifie que le dix-neuf du courant ont été inhumés au premier Camp d'en bas les corps de feu Jean Dugas et de Francois Arsenaud agé d'environ un an en foy de quoy j'ay signé aux Atakapas les jours et an que dessus et est signé F. Jean Francois, Curé.
Sep. Joseph Dugas	))	L'an mil sept cent soixante cinq, le 8, je, pretre Capucin Missionaire Apostolique, soussigné certifie que le six du présent mois a été inhumé au premier Camp d'en bas le corps de feu Joseph Dugas, en foy de quoy j'ai signé aux Atakapas le jour et an que dessus et est signé F. Jean Francois, Curé.
Sep. Magdelene Dugas	))	L'an Mil sept cent soixante cinq, je, pretre Capucin Missionaire Apostolique, Curé de la Nlle Acadie, certifie que le six du present mois a été inhumé le corps de feu Magdelene Dugas.

Record of the deaths of Alexandre Broussard and a Joseph Broussard.
Source: St. Martin of Tours Catholic Church Records (September 4, 1765).

and one in November, with different burial dates at different locations if both Joseph Broussards were the same person? I tend to think that there were two Joseph Broussards who died during that epidemic, one of them possibly a grandson of either the elder Joseph or his brother, Alexandre.

Therefore, it is unclear whether the burial records referred only to *Beausoleil* or possibly to another person named Joseph Broussard. A registry was made by Father Michel Bernard Barriere in 1796 from the original records, some of which were bound and others unbound.[61] In 2002, Arceneaux numbered each record and added helpful genealogical information in this registry supporting his belief that *Beausoleil* did not die on September 4th, but some unknown day before October 20, 1765. *Beausoleil's* entry is No. 36, to wit:

> *Broussard, Joseph dit Beau Soleil `Capitaine Commandat des Acadiens aux Attakapas' bur. 20 Oct. `au Camp appellé Beau Soleil'* recorded 25th of November.

In July, 1765, Grevemberg *dit* Flamm, an early colonial settler, filed a complaint that the Acadians were squatting on his land. It appears that the epidemic of 1765 prompted some of the *Beausoleil* Acadians to return to St. James Parish on the Mississippi River where they are noted in the census of April, 1766. By the early 1770s, the Acadians who had remained in the Attakapas had dispersed from their original settlements around present-day Loreauville to above present-day St. Martinville.[62] Later, some of the families relocated to Côte Gelée, near present-day Broussard, Louisiana, south of Bayou Tortue and also west of Breaux Bridge along the Vermilion River, and by the mid 1770s, from present-day Abbeville to north of Lafayette, an area known as the "Prairie de Vermilion."

Even after the death of *Beausoleil,* Acadians who remained either in Nova Scotia or Saint-Pierre and Miquelon islands continued to sail for Louisiana. On November 18, 1766, for instance, Commissioner Foucault wrote from New Orleans, "A month ago, 216 Acadians out of Halifax arrived here on an English ship rented at their own expense." [63] Dr. Carl A. Brasseaux opines that these Acadians were not from Halifax, but from Maryland.

In the earliest days, spellings of many words were highly personalized and not standardized as today, often in an attempt to reproduce spoken words phonetically. However, one attempt at standardization in 1820 Louisiana forever altered the spelling of most Acadian surnames ending in the sound of 'O'. In that year, Judge Paul Briant who was in charge of the U.S. census within the state arbitrarily chose the now-common 'eaux' ending for names like Boudreaux, Thibodeaux and Breaux, the last of which in Acadia was most often spelled "Braud."

Ironically, the judge directing the census in Louisiana was of French descent himself - and also a victim of violent displacement, having fled the slave-rebellion upheaval of Saint-Domingue, which is now called Haiti. Even though there are about a dozen alternatives in the French language to duplicate the phonetic ending, it was he who put the 'X' at the end of so many names. This action was to have a cultural consequence. During the years of ethnic humiliation in Louisiana, Acadians or "Cajuns" were convinced that the 'X' at the end of their surnames meant that their ancestors were illiterate and therefore had made a mark by their names in legal documents. While it was true that by modern standards there was a high degree of illiteracy on the frontiers of Canada and Louisiana, there was certainly no *less* literacy than in areas of English settlement where there was a correspondingly lower incidence of surname alteration. Tragically, the conventional wisdom that the 'X' at the end of a local surname indicates lower educational achievement among Cajun ancestors (and perhaps lower intelligence, too) still persists.

In 2003, in honor of the dedication of the Dispersion Cross at the Acadian Memorial in St. Martinville, Louisiana, James Louviere wrote the following lyrics for his song "O! O! Acadie!" which conveys what the Acadians must have felt upon arriving in New Acadia:

"Now the shadows of night gather round,
Foreign drums make their terrible sound,
They may tear us apart,
But they can't still the heart
Of your people, O sweet Acadie!

Will there be a new home, Acadie?
When we're scattered across every sea?
Will there ever again
Be a place in the sun
Where our hearts can live free, Acadie?

And the dénouement:

Acadie! Acadie! Acadie!
Our long, stormy night is no more!
Our desperate hope is fulfilled!
Here we rest, here we'll stay,
Evermore, all our days ....
This is truly our new Acadie!"

HEY, HEY, BEAUSOLEIL!

Dedicated to Joseph Broussard, leader of the resistance
To the British invasion of Acadie, now called "Nova Scotia"

Lively, with a bit of a military sound, snare drum, trumpet, flutes
(like Yankee Doodle, a little, or like a Sousa with the picollos)

Way-way back in his-t'ry there was a man
Who lead his faithful people to a pro-mised Land
He led his brave mi-li-tia on both land and sea,
Then he led them all to safety in new A-ca-die!

Hey, hey, Beausoleil,
They shot him and they jailed him
But he got away,
Oh, Oh! Great, Beausoleil,
We'll ne 'va ne 'va let yo' mem'ry fade away!

His wife and kids and brother and their fighting friends
Sailed along the Eastern Coast to Journey's end;
His people settled down around the Cote Gelee
And he led his people out of all their misery!

Hey, Hey, Beausoleil,
They shot him and they jailed him
But he got away,
Oh, Oh! Great Beausoleil,
We'll ne'va ne'va let yo' mem'ry fade away!

When the Cajuns were deported from their own sweet land,
There were a certain few with him who took a stand
They battled in the forests and they battled on the sea
And their family names are ringing, Living History!

Hey, Hey, Beausoleil,
They shot him and they jailed him
But he got away,
Oh, Oh! Great Beausoleil,
We'll ne'va ne'va let yo' mem'ry fade away

51

The winters were ferocious and the British foes were cruel
But Beausoleil's militia made 'em look like fools,
Until one final winter came with deep, deep snow,
He said, "Y'all get on my schooner, and away we go!"

They landed on an island where a fever struck,
So they sailed to Lou'siana and they had some luck
They ate some alligators and they caught nice fish
An' before you blink yo' eye they all appeared quite rich!

Their treasure wasn't money but deep in their hearts
They had the kind of lovin' that's still in these parts,
They had some real good families and some fine ol' songs
And the good times, they still roll along, real loud and long!

Hey, Hey, Beausoleil,
They shot him and they jailed him
But he got away,
Oh, Oh! Great Beausoleil,
We'll ne'va ne'va let yo' mem'ry fade away

We'll ne'va ne'va let yo' mem'ry fade a-way!

(solemn) (Chorus hums melody, Adult voice says....)
So all you little chil-dren who born and reared
Here in A-ca-di-an-a, where this man ap-peared,
Always keep these heroes in your memory,
Proudly <u>claim</u> the title "<u>Ca</u>jun - *from old A-ca-die!*"
(Children sing:) "Oh! We're <u>proud</u> we come from <u>Ca</u>juns from old A-ca-die!
　　　　　　　　Yes! We're ——<u>proud</u> we come from <u>Ca</u>juns from old A-ca-die!"

EVERYONE:
Hey, Hey, Beausoleil,
WE'LL KEEP YO' MEM'RY COOK-IN'
'TIL THE JUDGMENT DAY!
WE'LL KEEP YO' MEM'RY COOK-IN'
'TIL THE JUDGMENT DAY!

O, O! Acadie!

THE DAUTERIVE COMPACT:
THE FOUNDATION OF THE ACADIAN CATTLE INDUSTRY
Translated by Grover Rees

In the morning of this, the fourth day of April, 1765, before us, the undersigned royal notary of the province of Louisiana residing in New Orleans, there personally appeared *Antoine Bernard Dauterive*, a former infantry captain residing in this city, and *Joseph Broussard called Beausoleil, Alexandre Broussard, Joseph Guilbeau, Jean Duga, Olivier Tibaudau, Jean Baptiste Broussard, Pierre Arcenaud,* and *Victor Broussard,* Acadian chiefs also residing in this city.

In the presence of Mr. Charles Philip Aubry, knight of the Royal and Military Order of St. Louis and commandant of this colony, and of Mr. Denis-Nicolas Foucalt, acting *commissaire-ordonnateur* and first judge of the Superior Council of the said colony, they have agreed to the following:

Mr. Dauterive promises and obliges himself to furnish five cows with calves and one bull to each of the Acadian families during each of six consecutive years beginning on the day the animals are first delivered to the corral. The said Mr. Dauterive will bear the risk of loss of said cattle by death during the first year only, and he will replace them, if at all possible, without requiring the Acadians to share in this loss.

The said Mr. Dauterive reserves the right to terminate this partnership with the Acadians after three years counted from the date the Acadians first receive the animals and a division of the animals and their increase will then be made, sharing then equally.

The said Mr. Dauterive consents that the Acadians may sell a few cows or bulls, if they deem advisable, provided they keep an account of those they sell, which shall be verified by one of them (one of the eight Acadians).

This the said Acadians have accepted purely and simply and they have promised and obliged themselves to take care of the said cattle. At the end of said six years, they will each return the same number of cows and calves, of the same age and kind, that they received initially; the remaining cattle and their increase surviving at that time will be divided equally between said Acadians and Mr. Dauterive.

The abovenamed Acadians, acting individually and for their associates, obligate themselves and hypothecate their present and future property, individually and jointly, and Mr. Dauterive does likewise, hypothecating his property.

The above act was made and passed in New Orleans at the office of said Mr. Aubry on the abovementioned day, month, and year in the presence of Messrs. Leonard, Mazange, Curturier, the surgeon, witnesses residing here who have signed with Mr. Dauterive, the Acadians having declared that they did not know how to sign. This inquiry was done pursuant to the ordinance.

(signed) Aubry, Foucalt, Dauterive, Couturier, L. Mazange, de la Place (councillor assessor), and Garic, Notary

Officials:	Carles Philip Aubry, commandant
	Denis-Nicolas Foucalt, acting *commissaire- ordonnateur*
	Judge of the Superior Council
Participants:	Acadian family Chiefs
	Joseph Broussard called Beausoliel
	Alexendre Broussard
	Joseph Guilbeau
	Jean Duga
	Olivier Tibaudau
	Jean Baptist Broussard
	Pierre Arcenaud
	Victor Broussard
Witnesses:	Leonard, Mazange, Couturier
Notary:	Garic

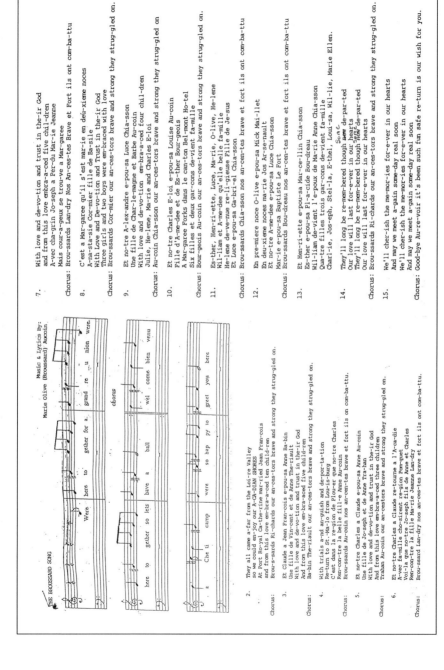

THE BROUSSARD SONG

Music & Lyrics By:
Marie Olive (Broussard) Aucoin

Were here to gether for a grand re u nion were
here to gether so lets have a ball wel come bien venu
chorus
Che ti camp were so hap py to greet you here

2. They all came a-far from the Loi-re Valley
so we could en-joy our A-CA-DIAN SHORES
At Fort Ro-yal Ca-the-rine mar-ried Jean Fran-cois
and from this love em-bra-a-ced ten child-ren
Brou-ssards Ri-chards our an-ces-tors brave and strong they strug-gled on.

Chorus:

3. Et Claude a Jean Fran-cois e-pou-sa Anne Ba-bin
Une fille de Vin-cent et de Anne The-ri-ault
With love and de-vo-tion and trust in the-ir God
And from this love em-bra-aced five child-ren
Ba-bin The-ri-ault our an-ces-tors brave and strong they strug-gled on.

Chorus:

4. With trials a-nd au-guish and de-por-ta-tion
Re-turn to St. Ma-lo from Lou-is-burg
C'est dans la re-gion de Plou-er que no-tre Charles
Ren-con-tre la belle fill-e Anne Au-coin
Brou-ssards Au-coin nos an-cen-tes brave et fort ils on com-ba-ttu.

Chorus:

5. Et no-tre Charles a Claude e-pou-sa Anne Au-coin
Une fille de Jo-seph et de Anne Tra-han
With love and de-vo-tion and trust in the-ir God
And from this love em-bra-a-ced three children
Trahan Au-coin our an-cestors brave and strong they strug-gled on.

Chorus:

6. Et no-tre Charles a Claude re-tourne a l'A-ca-die
A-vec fa-mille cho-sirent re-gion Pom-quet
Voi-la que no-tre Jo-seph fils de Anne et Charles
Ren-con-tre la fille Ma-rie Jeanne Lan-dry
Brou-ssard Lan-dry nos an-ces-tes brave et fort ils ont com-ba-ttu.

Chorus:

7. With love and de-vo-tion and trust in the-ir God
and from this love embra-a-ced five chil-dren
A-vec cha-grin Jo-seph a Per-du Mar-ie Jeanne
Mais cour-a-geux se trou-ve a Mar-garee
Chorus: Brou-ssards Lan-dry Nos An-ces-tes Brave et Fort ils ont com-ba-ttu

8. C'est a Mar-garee qu'il s'est mar-ie en deu-xieme noces
A-na-sta-sie Cor-mier fille de Ba-sile
With Love and De-vo-tion and Trust in the-ir God
Three girls and two boys were em-braced with love
Chorus: Brou-ssards Cor-mier our an-ces-tors brave and strong they strug-gled on.

9. Et no-tre A-lex-andre e-pou-sa Luce Chia-sson
Une fille de Char-le-magne et Barbe Au-coin
With love and de-vo-tion em-bra-a-ced four chil-dren
Julie, He-lene, Ma-rie and Charles E-loi
Chorus: Au-coin Chia-sson our an-ces-tors brave and strong they strug-gled on

10. Et no-tre Charles E-loi e-pou-sa Louise Au-coin
Fille d'A-me-dee et de Es-ther Bour-geois
A Mar-garee Forks dans le can-ton Bel-mont Ho-tel
Six filles et deux gar-cons de-vient fa-mille
Chorus: Bour-geois Au-coin our an-ces-tors brave and strong they strug-gled on.

11. Es-ther, Hen-ri-ette, Luce, Ma-rie, O-live, He-lene
Wil-liam et A-me-dee qu'elle belle fa-mille
He-lene de-ve-nue re-li-gieuse Fille de Je-sus
Et Luce e-pou-sa Ga-bri-el Chia-sson
Chorus: Brou-ssards Chia-sson nos an-cen-tes brave et fort ils ont com-ba-ttu

12. En pre-miere noce O-live e-pou-sa Mick Mai-llet
En deu-xieme noces ma-rie Jos Ar-se-nault
Et no-tre A-me-dee e-pou-sa Luce Chia-sson
Mar-ie e-pou-sa Baptiste Le Fort
Chorus: Brou-ssards Bou-dreau nos an-ces-tes brave et fort ils ont com-ba-ttu

13. Et Hen-ri-ette e-pou-sa Mar-ce-llin Chia-sson
Es-ther e-pou-sa Pl-a-cide Bou-dreau
Wil-liam de-vient l'e-poux de Ma-rie Anne Chia-sson
Qua-tre filles trois gar-cons de-vient fa-mille
Charl-ie, Jos-eph, Stel-la, E-thel, Loui-sa, Wil-lie, Marie Ellen.

14. They'll long be re-mem-bered though now de-par-ted
Our love will last for-e-ver in our hearts
They'll long be re-mem-bered though now de-par-ted
Our love will last for-e-ver in our hearts
Chorus: Brou-ssards Ri-chards our an-ces-tors brave and strong they strug-gled on.

15. We'll cher-ish the me-mor-ies for-e-ver in our hearts
And may we meet a-gain some-day real soon
We'll cher-ish the me-mor-ies for-e-ver in our hearts
And may we meet a-gain some-day real soon
Chorus: Good-bye Au-re-voir it's been such fun safe re-turn is our wish for you.

CHAPTER 8
THE LEGACY

*B*eausoleil's cultural impact upon today's Cajuns is impressive. His favorable character traits are immortalized in music, art, poetry, novels and folklore.

Beausoleil emerged from the Acadian expulsion as the only Acadian folk hero. Pro-British historians have referred to Broussard as "an indefatigable foe." In an effort to show her admiration, Canadian Marie Olive Broussard Aucoin, a native of Cheticamp, Nova Scotia, wrote "The Broussard Song." (see page 52)

The main exhibit in the Acadian Room at the Acadian Museum of Erath is called "*Beausoleil* - Chief of the Acadians." The highlight of the exhibit is a three by five foot painting entitled "*Beausoleil.*" Joseph "Jimmie" Hebert was the model for the painting by renowned muralist Robert Dafford, which was donated to the Acadian Museum by Hebert's daughters, Theresa Hebert Vincent and Patricia Hebert Marks. Lucius Fontenot, an artist from Mamou, Louisiana, now living in Lafayette, Louisiana, drew an image of a young *Beausoleil* (see book cover), which was placed upon T-shirts to appeal to younger upcoming generations, and which are now being sold to support the Acadian Museum of Erath[64].

Acclaimed musician and poet Zachary Richard used references to *Beausoleil* in his anthem "Réveille," written in 1973. The song was first recorded in 1976 on the album *Bayou des Mystères.* The song was again recorded in 2000 on the album *Coeur Fidèle,* and used in the soundtrack of the award-winning film *Against the Tide* by Pat Mire:

> *J'ai entendu parler*
> *De monter avec Beausoleil.*
> *Pour prendre le fusil*
> *Battre les sacrés maudits.*
> *J'ai entendu parlér*
> *D'aller dans la Louisianne*
> *Pour trouver de la bonne paix*
> *Là-bas dans la Louisianne.*

In 1978, Richard also recorded "La Ballade de *Beausoleil*" on the album *Migration:*

> *La lune est pleine, on monte ce soir avec Beausoleil.*
> *Il fera claire au fond du grand bois.*
> *Déjà les hommes ils sont fatigués,*
> *L'hiver passé on n'était pas capable de se loger.*
> *De plus en plus on parle de la Louisianne.*
> *Ce n'était rien qu'un rêve qu'on appellait l'Acadie.*

In Richard's award-winning album *Cap Enragé*, he recorded the song "Petit Codiac," which was based upon the poem written by Yves Chaisson. The lyrics read: "Crazy Horse, *Beausoleil*, Louis Riel, Jackie

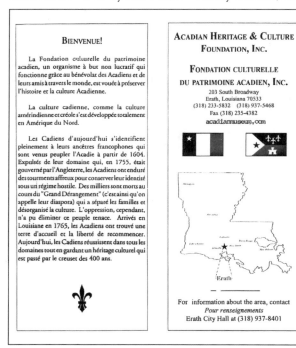

Vautour, *Asteur c'est mon tour.*" Yves Chaisson here is equating *Beausoleil* with other important historical figures.

According to Acadian Memorial Director, Brenda Comeaux Trahan, when the Acadian Memorial was opened in St. Martinville on April 29,

1996, the event was highlighted by a dramatic portrayal of "*Beausoleil*" by Francophone actor Shirley Savoy. His soliloquy was written by Dr. Barry Ancelet, former head of the Modern Languages department, University of Louisiana at Lafayette. Today, the role is being played by Richard Landry. The main attraction at the Acadian Memorial is a twelve by thirty foot mural painted by Robert Dafford. It is titled "The Arrival of the Acadians in Louisiana." The central character in the mural is "*Beausoleil*" (see mural on page 60).

Beausoleil's name was appropriated by the modern Louisiana Cajun Band, led by Michael Doucet, that won a Grammy in 1997. The rebel's name also appears in many historical novels such as Claude LeBouthillier's *Le Feu du Mauvais Temps* (1989), J. Alphonse Devau's, *Le Chef des Acadiens*[65] (1980) and Antonine Maillet's *Pélagie-la-Charrette* (1970). The former freedom-fighter has become a mesmerizing figure in Acadian history.

In Maillet's *Pélagie*, an award-winning novel set in the 1770s, "*Beausoleil*" is portrayed as a captain of a ship, the *Grande Coule*, who transports Acadians to be reunited with their families. The book represents a combination of imagination and folklore. It is also an example of Acadian expression and attitudes of the times.[66] Maillet writes:

> Alive! Captain Broussard, Broussard-called *Beausoleil* – master of an English four-master rechristened *Grande Goule* and a full crew of survivors ... Aye, Bélonie, survivors, survivors from midocean snatched from the furious sea and their pitiless jailers by none other than *Beausoleil*, another deported Acadian. And *Beausoleil*-Broussard himself, alive in body and soul, jumps to the quai at *Pélagie's* feet and presents his ship to the cart. One after another the sailors leap ashore and shake the shoulders of their countrymen, neighbors and cousins ...

Just as Maillet's fictionalized "*Beausoleil*" worked to reunite Acadians in Canada, his real-life descendants in Louisiana organized *La Famille Beausoleil Association* using his name to reunite over 10,000 Broussards during the *Congrès Mondial Acadien Louisiane* in 1999 in Broussard, Louisiana.[67] Also, under the leadership of President Brian Comeaux, there were ninety other Acadian family reunions sponsored by the

Congrès Mondial Acadien Louisiane.

In Bliss Carman's poem *"The Vengeance of Noel Brassard - A Tale of the Acadian Expulsion," "Beausoleil"* is shadowed by "Walker of the Snow:"

"Ah, *Beausoleil,* before you now The Wilderness; and by your side The shadowy Walker of the Snow, To journey with you, stride for stride, On many a drifted valley floor!" [68]

The latest literary effort portraying *Beausoleil* is the historical novel *Three Hills Home,* by award-winning Nova Scotian novelist Alfred Silver. In the "Author's Notes," Silver writes: "The one central character who isn't a patchwork creation is *Beausoleil.*" The opening lines of the book dramatically introduce *"Beausoleil":*

In a South Louisiana town stands a blood-grained granite monument to a man who died two centuries before it was carved and who lived almost all of his life a thousand miles north. The British of his day called him an outlaw, a murderer and a pirate. The French called him a patriot and the founder of New Acadia. But one thing neither his friends nor his enemies called him was his baptized name, which was Joseph Brossard. They called him *Beausoleil.*" [69]

"THE ARRIVAL OF THE ACADIANS IN LOUISIANA"©

THE ACADIAN MEMORIAL
A monument to Louisiana's Acadian legacy
EVANGELINE OAK PARK
ST. MARTINVILLE, LOUISIANA

According to Vaughn Madden, *Directrice Générale* of the *Congrès*

Mondial Acadien 2004, as part of the activities of the *Congrès* there was a "Beausoleil Day" celebrated on August 5, 2004, at the Forchu Festival 2004 in Yarmouth, Nova Scotia. Organizer of the festival, Reg LeBlanc, said that the annual event was organized to honor the man who "was a freedom fighter for the Acadians."

Although *Beausoleil* led many of his people to "New Acadia," he died before he could enjoy the fruits of his struggle and perseverance. *Beausoleil* is still revered today, particularly by Acadians in Louisiana[70] for whom he has become a legendary figure for his bravery as leader of the resistance of the Acadians in Nova Scotia and the "Chief" of the Broussard clan in Louisiana.

In the Glen Pitre movie *Belizaire - The Cajun*, filmed in 1985, *Belizaire* is a supposed "wise man" and *traiteur* who is played by actor Armand Assante. Ironically, *Belizaire* is always in trouble. The theme of the movie: if *Belizaire* is so smart, why is he always in so much trouble? That theme conjures up the complex man *Beausoleil*. Much more was unearthed about him from historical records than any other Acadian. It is believed that whatever was said or written about him, be it good or bad, had a tinge of truth to it. He was just sometimes a mediator, other times a militant; engrossing yet maddening; dominant yet yielding, and admirable yet blameworthy.

Some have elevated *Beausoleil* to mythic status. Yet when one revisits his life, we indeed find a man larger than life, an authentic (in an older sense) man of a time and place who was thrown into brutal and humiliating circumstances that tested his courage, perseverance and survival skills. Just as he had a reputation as a sharpshooter, he was also known in peacetime as a "hothead," easily drawn to violence. Later, he was delivered into circumstances devoid of lawfulness and reason; violence begat violence, and thus are born our mythical heros. At times the British authorities found him villainous, and at other times conciliatory. The one thing upon which everyone agrees was that he never withdrew from his goal: to prevent the Acadian culture from being assimilated into the British culture. To that end, he never wavered from his commitment.

Did he succeed in his goal? When faced with the prospect of remaining in Nova Scotia and being assimilated into British culture, he chose the courageous, bold and fearless path: voluntary expatriation. As an *émigré*, he saw the opportunity to continue the Acadian culture in a more politically hospitable, yet ironically harsher environment - Louisiana. Today, his memory and vision live on. He must be viewed as a complex, paradoxical icon.

Beausoleil's determination to prevent cultural assimilation can be found in his descendants who today continue to work to save the French language in Louisiana. Great care should be taken in the saving of minority languages because the history of a people is always encoded in the language they speak. Things such as traditions, folklore, world view, religious beliefs, genealogy, and even food production methods and land use management are embedded in Cajun French, their colloquialisms and idiomatic expressions. Within the French language of south Louisiana are traces of the facts that these French speakers have lived in close contact with many other ethnic populations: with the early Spanish settlers of the region, with the local Native American population, with their Creole French-speaking neighbors, and finally, with the last-to-arrive English-speaking Americans. There are idiomatic expressions that include the fact that it was once possible to obtain land grants from the Spanish government in Louisiana, that hunting, trapping, farming and fishing were once important occupations. There are succulent dishes on dinner tables in South Louisiana with Indian and African names. If we lose the Louisiana French language, we lose a treasure trove of history.

It is hoped that *Beausoleil's* descendants will take note of the warning given by Dr. Shane K. Bernard in the conclusion of his recent book, *The Cajuns - Americanization of a People:*

> Ultimately, the future of the Cajun people remains unclear. They may succumb entirely to the process of Americanization or stagger along indefinitely on the edge of extinction, or they may rebound, flowering in a new Age of Ethnicity. Regardless, the almost instinctive ability of the Cajuns to swim in the mainstream will assure their survival for at least a few more generations. No matter their language or culture or where they find themselves, it is hoped that these new generations will devoutly heed the inscription found beside the Acadian Memorial's eternal flame. *"Un peuple sans passé est un peuple sans future"* – A people without a past are a people without a future.[71]

Beausoleil was a provocative warrior who had a never-say-die spirit. Myths about him abound: he could not hear a Yankee name pronounced without being sent into a frenzy. He proudly notched the butt of his weapon to mark the killing of a British soldier; when he died there were twenty-eight notches on his rifle. It must be noted, however, that not all of his exploits are recorded in the archives.[72]

In 2005, Acadians will commemorate the 250th anniversary of the deportation of the Acadians. Karl J. Hakla, Acadian Unit Manager, Jean Lafitte National Park and Preserve, Acadian Culture Center in Lafayette, Louisiana, is organizing various events. At his request, Georgette LeBlanc, an Acadian from Nova Scotia who is pursuing a Ph.D. in Francophone Studies at the University of Louisiana at Lafayette, has written a play, one of whose main characters is *Beausoleil*. Ms. LeBlanc wrote the following in her project description which fittingly describes the Louisiana Acadian culture:

> The deportation separated extended families, friends and lovers. Acadians were, as Carl Brasseaux beautifully says it, like 'seeds scattered to the wind.' If we are commemorating the deportation in Lafayette, Louisiana in August, 2005, two hundred and fifty years later, it is justly because thousands of these seeds took root in Louisiana's watery soil. These seeds have grown to become what is now celebrated the world over as Cajun culture. A vibrant and musical one indeed.

What will it take to keep the Cajun culture strong and alive in the years to come? The Acadians and Mi'Kmaq formed an enduring friendship and alliance in Acadia. We can still learn much from the Mi'Kmaq's experience, particularly with cultural assimilation. Today, L'sitkuk (pronounced elsetkook) people are part of the Mi'Kmaq First Nation and are called the Bear River Mi'Kmaq. They have lived in Nova Scotia's Digby and Annapolis counties for thousands of years. The disruptive effects of the European settlers profoundly affected the people who were the first Mi'Kmaq to have continuous contact with the Europeans. Nestled close to the Bear River watershed, this tiny native community is regaining its culture, language and identity. As in the past, the Acadians and Mi'Kmaq are continuing to seek cultural autonomy. The challenge is proudly summarized by the present Chief of the L'sitkuk, Chief Frank Meuse, Jr., on the cover of the book, *Lísitkuk - The Story of the Bear River Mi'Kmaw Community*, by Darlene A. Ricker: "We have endured slavery, starvation, genocide and wars, but the spirit of our people has survived. We have one battle left to fight - ourselves."

Leurs mains se touchèrent.

Source: J. Alphonse Deveau, *Le Chef Des Acadiens* (Lescarbot, Yarmouth, Nova Scotia, 1980) p. 119.

ACADIAN GUERRILLAS — Under the leadership of the two "Beausoleils," Alexandre and Joseph Broussard, a small band of Acadians conducted guerrilla warfare against the British after the dispersal of the Acadians. The British soldiers con- fiscated the farms, homes and other property of the Acadians, who refused to swear allegiance to the English king. (Drawing by Mary Lenny Perrin)

Source: Mary B. Perrin, *Were Early Acadian Men Really the Docile Type?*, *The Daily Advertiser*, November, 1977.

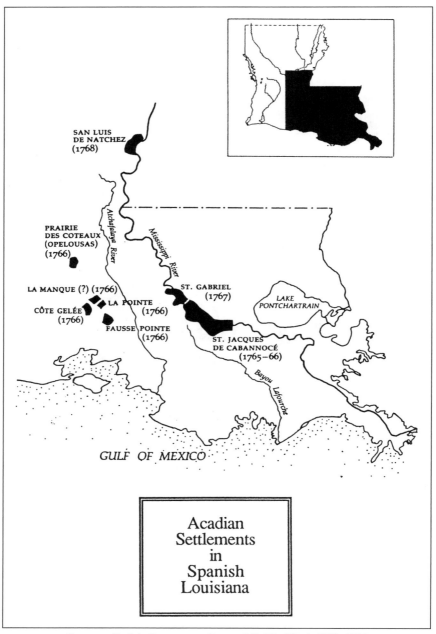

SAN LUIS
DE NATCHEZ
(1768)

PRAIRIE
DES COTEAUX
(OPELOUSAS)
(1766)

Atchafalaya River

Mississippi River

LA MANQUE (?) (1766)

LA POINTE
(1766)

CÔTE GELÉE
(1766)

FAUSSE POINTE
(1766)

ST. GABRIEL
(1767)

LAKE
PONTCHARTRAIN

ST. JACQUES
DE CABANNOCÉ
(1765–66)

Bayou Lafourche

GULF OF MEXICO

Acadian
Settlements
in
Spanish
Louisiana

Source: Carl A. Brasseaux, *Scattered To The Wind, 1755–1809*
(USL Center for Louisana Studies, 1991).

CHAPTER 9
THE BROUSSARD CLAN IN LOUISIANA

The Broussards today comprise one of the state's largest clans of French origin.[73] The name is rare in the Acadian regions of the maritimes of Canada, but the name lives on in Quebec, where a significant number of family members found refuge after the deportation. More than half of the Broussards in the state of Louisiana still live in the area of Bayou Teche, part of the old district of Attakapas where their ancestors, refugees from Acadia, settled 250 years ago. In 1952, Harry Lewis Griffin, Dean Emeritus of the College of Liberal Arts, now the University of Louisiana at Lafayette, then Southwestern Louisiana Institute, described the Acadians migration to the area as follows:

> These families were housed in temporary camps until they could be assigned to lands by the commandants in charge. These newcomers were welcomed by the French and Spanish authorities and given every assistance in securing suitable farms on which to settle and start life anew. From 1765 to 1780, and especially from 1765 to 1788, there was a steady influx of these Acadians coming from San Domingo, Guiana, the ports of New England and from France where many of them had found temporary refuge. From these centers these industrious people gradually spread out into south and southwest Louisiana where they, for many years to come, formed the basic population of that area. By 1780, Acadians numbered 2,500; by 1790, 4,000 and by 1900 between 40,000 and 50,000. Here in their new homes they engaged in farming and cattle-raising on a large scale as they had done in Acadia; and diligently preserved their customs, traditions and language with the greatest fidelity.[74]

As a result of the Dauterive Compact, the Broussard brothers began the occupation that was to become the mark of many Broussards and other Acadian families of southwest Louisiana: the raising of cattle. Although both *Beausoleil* and Alexandre died shortly after their arrival, by the 1770's several of their sons had firmly established the Broussard name in the Attakapas territory.

Even though Louisiana was officially a Spanish colony in the late eighteenth century, the French government continued to exert considerable influence and sent newly arriving Acadians to the *Poste des Attakapas* district and also to the Opelousas district. The Opelousas district included the present-day parishes of St. Landry, Acadia, Jeff Davis, Calcasieu, Cameron, Beauregard, Allen and Evangeline.

It was not until 1769 that the Spanish government officially took control of the territory with their own governor and the Spanish flag eventually flew over all of Louisiana, including the Attakapas territories. The ethnic parameters of this Louisiana colonial complex expanded during the three decades of Spanish sovereignty to include Acadians, Canary Islanders, French refugees from the Haitian Revolt, a considerable number of enslaved Africans, and, notably, English-speaking settlers in large numbers.[75] Louis Andry, a surveyor and military engineer who accompanied the Acadians to the area, received instructions from the Governor to work with *Beausoleil* to lay out a village with a common area. The land beyond the common area was to be distributed to the Acadians in parcels sized according to the size of their families. The obstinate Acadians ignored the plan. They settled on widely separated tracts of land.

The initial land holdings of the Broussards extended from St. Martinville on the Bayou Teche westward to Bayou Vermilion, including part of the rolling Côte Gelée where the first Acadian settlement was made at Camp Beausoleil.[76] As early as 1766, one year after their arrival, some of *Beausoleil's* sons had established households within the section then called Bayou Tortue between the Teche and Vermilion rivers. *Beausoleil's* other children who settled the area were Raphael (married Rose LeBlanc in 1754), Joseph *dit P'tit Joseph* (married Anastasie LeBlanc in 1755 and Marguerite Savoie in 1767), and Amand (married Helene Landry in 1771 and Anne Benoit in 1775). Three sons - and possibly two grandsons - of Alexandre settled near the Teche at La Pointe above St. Martinville. By 1774, most Broussard families had acquired fairly large herds of cattle, as well as horses and hogs.

When the hostilities began between the American colonists and Britain, the Acadians saw an opportunity for long-awaited retribution against the British. Louisiana Acadian militiamen, along with whatever other soldiers the Spanish Governor Bernardo de Galvez could round up, took Mobile, Pensacola, Baton Rouge and Natchez from the English

L'an mille sept cent soixante treze & le seizieme jour du [...] de may a trois heures
apres midy les habitants des Atakapas s'etant assemblé pour proceder a l'election d'un
second Sindic pour aider le Sr. Berard dans la repartition des bois de L'eglise & dans
toutes les operations qui y auront apport ainsi que le recouvrement des deniers du a
l'entrepreneur pour la main d'oeuvre de L'eglise. Les voix de tous les habitants ci
presens aiant eté recueillies, tous d'un commun accord ont nommé le Sr. Louis Armand
Ducrest pour adjoin de Sieur Berard ci-devant elu sindic & de nouveau approuvé &
convenu par tous les habitants denommés dans le presens proces verbal. Les quels ont
signé & fait signer pour eux, ainsi que nous commandant du district aux Atakapas les
susdits jour, mois & an que sudessus.

Labbee   Sorrel   Collete   Martin Poke   Fuselier de la Clair

Francois Ducuir
Pour
5 Claude Martin   19 J. Bte. Broussard   33 Fran. Broussard
6 Olivier Thibodeau   20 Simond Broussard   34 Jean Dugas
7 Amant Thibodeau   21 Jean Trahan   35 Charles Dugas
8 Paul Thibodeau   22 Pierre Naiza   36 Baptiste la Beuve
9 Fran. Guillebeau   23 Firmin Landry   37 Pierre Dugas
10 Michel Bernard   24 Jean Labbé, fils   38 Amant Broussard
11 Simond le blanc   25 Vincent Barras   39 Anselme Thibodeau
12 Charles Guillebeau   26 Nicolas Prevost   40 Claude Broussard
13 Charles Babino   27 Jos. Prevost   41 René Trahan
14 Philipe Wilz   28 Martin Soudric   42 Michel Mo
15 Joseph Wilz   29 Michel Trahan   43 Antoine Bonin
16 Joseph Hebert   30 Joseph Broussard   44 Jean Louis Bonin
17 Pierre Broussard   31 J. Bte. Seymer   45 Paul Trahan
18 Silvain Broussard   32 J. Bte. Hebert   46 Jean Charles Hebert
                                                   47 Pierre Porche

Les Sieurs Borda & Boutté ont nommé le Sr. Louis Grevemberg
Signé Bouttet   Borda

Messiers Delahoussaye & deVaugine ont nommé pour sindic & aussi par la main du
Sr. la couronne J. Bte. Bessiere nous disans qu'ils ont nommé le Sr. Jean Baptiste
Grevemberg.
Pour Messrs. de la Houssaye et Vaugine   Bessiere

Le Sr. Louis Grevemberg a nommé pour sindic le Sr. Boutté, fils ainé.
Signé Louis Grevember

Vu les signatures ci dessus & apres avoir compté les voix & prouvé que la pluralité de
quarante sept voix avait choisi le Sr. Armand Ducrest, nous avons determiné qu'il
demeurerait sindic & adjoin du Sr. Berard.
Atakapas le 16 may 1773.

                              Fuselier de la Clair

        The undersigned, Clerk of Court of the Parish of St. Martin, State of Louisiana,
hereby certifies that the foregoing is a correct typewritten copy of an act signed on
May 16, 1773 by Fuselier de la Clair, Commandant of the District of Attakapas, and by
others, announcing the election of Louis Armand Ducrest as assistant sindic for the
construction of the church, as said act appears recorded in Volume 1, (1760-1779) of
Original Acts kept in the office of the Clerk of Court of said parish.

                              R. A. Barras, Clerk of Court of St. Martin Parish

        Note: This document, signed by Gabriel Fuselier de la Clair, Commandant of the
Attakapas, and by others on May 16, 1773 should be of historical interest because
it establishes the year of construction of the first church building at the
Poste des Attakapas and contains the names of 53 contributing parishioners who, it
may be assumed, were all heads of families. This compares with the 73 heads of
families listed in the October 30, 1774 Census of the whole district of Attakapas
taken by the then commandant, Chevalier Alexandre Declouet, for the Spanish
Government. Grover Rees.

Document which authorizes the first church in the Attakapas territories.

during the American Revolution. These actions qualified participating Acadian militiamen to be patriots of the American Revolution. Many of these Acadians' names are enshrined today on a plaque in Acadian Village in Lafayette, Louisiana.

In 1773, Gabriel Fuselier de la Clair was the Commandant of the District of Attakapas. On May 16, 1773, de la Clair signed a document affirming the agreement among fifty-three Acadians to construct the first Church at the *Poste des Attakapas* in what is now present-day St. Martinville, Louisiana. These signees were probably heads of the families in the area. The October 30, 1774, census reported seventy-three heads of families in the Attakapas District according to the then Spanish Commandant, Chevalier Alexandre Declouet.[77]

In the 1820s, the Broussards were concentrated primarily in three areas all near the site of the initial settlement: at Fausse Point on Bayou Teche near present-day New Iberia where sixteen families had farms; along the Vermilion River in Lafayette and Vermilion parishes where there were thirteen farms and in Côte Gelée near the city of Broussard where there were five established families. In addition, three families lived along the Bayou Teche at Grand Pointe near present-day Breaux Bridge, two near St. Martinville, three along Bayou Petite Anse near Avery Island and one each at Lake Peigneur (Iberia Parish) and Prairie Sorrel.

In the nineteenth century, these families probably raised food crops, indigo and sugarcane. In 1812, Alexander's son, Pierre Broussard (married Marie Mélançon in 1776), worked his plantation on the Bayou Teche with forty-two slaves. His cousin, *Beausoleil's* son, Amand (married Hélène Landry in 1771), had twenty-two slaves at Fausse Point. Up until the Civil War, several Broussard families continued as planters along the Bayou Teche. However, the descendants of Pierre maintained the old family plantation "Marie Louise" at Fausse Point well into the twentieth century. The Broussards who settled along the Vermilion River, like many of their neighbors, engaged in both farming and livestock. During the last quarter of the eighteenth century, several Broussard families obtained property along the lower Vermilion River north of present-day Abbeville. For example, *Beausoleil's* son, François (married Pélagie Landry in 1770) and Claude (married Louise Hébert in 1772) had settled there in the late 1780's. François claimed a large prairie tract of 1,000 acres as a *vacherie*, or cattle ranch. By 1850, Vermilion

CATTLE BRANDING IN SOUTHWEST LOUISIANA · 115

SOME BRANDS FROM THE BOOK OF BRANDS FOR THE DISTRICTS OF
OPELOUSAS AND ATTAKAPAS, 1760–1888 (Plate II)

#	Brand	Description	#	Brand	Description
1	10 7	Boutte' Louis Hilaire, homme de couleur libre, St. Martin Jan. 17, 1817, p. 13	15		Chevallier Declouet St. Martin, June 1, 1780 p. 40
2	℮B	Paul Pierre Briant St. Martin, July 20, 1821 p. 15	16	Œ+	Declouet Chevalier fils d'Alexandre, St. Martin June 18, 1784, p. 43
3	☆	Briant Pierre Paul St. Martin, Oct. 9, 1824 p. 15	17	∩4	Martin Duralde St. Martin, Mar. 12, 1789 p. 46
4	J♭	Louis Maduse (Spaniard) St. Martin, July 14, 1827 p. 17	18	mo	Modist Delahoussay, f.w.c. St. Martin, July 12, 1814 p. 47
5	JPL	Catin, Negresse Libre passed to Louis La Violette, June 13, 1808, St. Martin, p. 24	19		François Quarteren Libre St. Martin, May 29, 1792 p. 57
6	♂S	Celestin Sauvage Attakapas St. Landry, June 13, 1808 p. 24	20	5F	Louis Grevemberg St. Martin, Oct. 14, 1793 p. 64
7	2b	Celestin Sauvage Attakapas St. Martin, Aug. 18, 1804 p. 29	21	FR	François Grevemberg St. Martin, Oct. 14, 1770 p. 64
8	✠	Chaulinette Quarteren Libre St. Martin, Aug. 12, 1805 p. 30	22	Z3	Josephe, Mitif Libre St. Martin, Aug. 4, 1800 p. 81
9	I'N	Charlotte, Nsse Libre St. Martin, July 26, 1815 p. 33	23	ꝺ	Jos. Mathew, Griffe Libre St. Landry, Oct. 7, 1822 p. 98
10	JL	Chataign Sauvage St. Martin 1826 p. 33	24	⅄	Melançon Veuve St. Martin, Sept. 21, 1801, p. 105
11	PS	Dermancourt Joseph Sauvage St. Landry, Aug. 4, 1825 p. 108	25	⌐	Belthazare Martel St. Martin, July 16, 1823 p. 108
12	D.C	Chevalier Declouet St. Martin, June 1, 1770 p. 40	26	FXM	F. X. Martin St. Martin, Sept. 1, 1823 p. 108
13	D.C	Declouet Vve. St. Martin, June 1, 1776 p. 40	27	ID	Ozenne pere St. Martin, Oct. 14, 1748 p. 113
14	GP	Gonealan Deprades St. Martin, Mar. 1, 1780 p. 40	28	ID	Ozenne Jacques Pyois pere, St. Martin, Aug. 13, 1748, p. 113

Source: *Cattle Brands of the Acadien and Early Settlers of Louisiana/Attakapas*
Glenda Shoeffler (1992).

ADDITIONAL BRANDS FROM THE BOOK OF BRANDS FOR THE DISTRICTS OF
OPELOUSAS AND ATTAKAPAS, 1760–1888 (Plate III)

#	Brand	Owner	#	Brand	Owner
1	ID7	Ozenne Usin son fils St. Martin, Sept. 11, 1802 p. 113	15	P	Gilbert Handy, fils freedman, St. Landry, Aug. 28, 1866, p. 407
2	AP	Alexander Porter St. Martin, Aug. 16, 1809 p. 118	16	(brand)	Marie Thibedeaux freedwoman, St. Martin, July 29, 1867, p. 421
3	WK	William Wikoff St. Landry, June 29, 1815 p. 150	17	(brand)	Edmond Senegal, col. Lafayette, July 31, 1869, p. 443
4	≠	Lemlette f.w.c. St. Martin, Aug. 23, 1830 p. 168	18	(brand)	Philomene Gautraut Lafayette, Nov. 16, 1872, p. 494
5	(brand)	Marie Louise Senegal, f.w.c. Lafayette, Apr. 9, 1840 p. 217	19	3	John McNeese Calcasieu, Nov. 29, 1873, p. 501
6	SUC	Sebastian Hernandez Lafayette, April 10, 1844 p. 257	20	WARE	John M. Ware St. Landry, May 25, 1883, p. 588
7	(brand)	John Hanks Vermilion, Aug. 27, 1844 p. 240	21	(brand)	Joseph Jefferson Iberia, July 21, 1887 p. 613
8	(brand)	Desire'Migues St. Martin, Aug. 21, 1857 p. 279	22	4D	Domingue Caesar Acadia, June 13, 1888 p. 618
9	(brand)	Seathene Schixmayder Vermilion, Sept. 10, 1855 p. 310	23	4O	Joseph Breaux Acadia, June 13, 1888 p. 618
10	HA	Louis Attakapas St. Landry p. 332	24	4H	Alphonse Broussard St. Martin, June 14, 1888 p. 618
11	(brand)	Baptiste Mulatre Libre St. Landry, Sept. 4, 1815 p. 338	25	4K	Geo. K. Bradford Acadia, Aug. 29, 1888 p. 620
12	(brand)	Bernard Chef Attakapas St. Martin, Apr. 18, 1801 p. 343	26	aH	Aladin Hanks Acadia, Aug. 11, 1888 p. 620
13	(brand)	Joseph Green Senegal, f.m.c. Lafayette, Aug. 15, 1866 p. 406	27	4H	Levigne Comeaux Acadia, July 21, 1888 p. 619
14	(brand)	Leocadie St. Andre, f.p.c. St. Landry, Aug. 30, 1866 p. 407	28	42	Alcide Richard Lafayette, June 30, 1888 p. 619

Some brands from the Book of Brands for the Districts of Opelousas
and Attakapas, 1760–1888. The format used here is that of the modern Book
of Brands for Louisiana, 1955. Note that early recordings are in French,
and the later ones are in English. Gilbert Handy, fils freedman, shows as
being transitional. The great majority of listings were those of white cattle-
men; these are among the unusual designations and may be of interest for
a variety of reasons. Note that Indians and colored people usually were
listed by a single name.

CATTLE BRANDING IN SOUTHWEST LOUISIANA 117

SOME BRANDS FROM THE LOUISIANA BRAND BOOK, 1955 (Plate IV)

#	Brand	Owner	Side	Brand	Owner	Side	#
1	L	Earl K. Long Winfield	L	LA	La. State Penitentiary Angola	R	15
2	W	Noah Ward 6821 Government St. Baton Rouge	R	LU	Animal Indus. Dept. LSU Univ. Station Baton Rouge	L	16
3	⌐P	David L. Pearce Oak Grove	R	L6	La. Ag. Exp. Station Box 8877 Univ. Sta. Baton Rouge	L	17
4	IHH	Ike Hamilton 210 Thompson St. West Monroe	R	SP	La. State Police Baton Rouge	R	18
5	III	George P. Gayden, Jr. Gurley	L	−LS	Southwestern La. Inst. Lafayette	L	19
6	△	J. M. Petitjean 131 Harrison St. Lake Charles	L	C+C	St. Charles College Grand Coteau	R	20
7	HB	W. H. Beene, Jr. Box 5218 Bossier City	L	†	St. Gertrude's Convent Ramsey	R	21
8	HT−	H. C., S. and Herman Taylor, Jr. Natchitoches	R	SJA	St. Joseph's Abbey St. Benedict	R	22
9	◇	R. Watkins Greene R. F. D. Youngsville	R	HP	Harry Post Luling	R	23
10	〰	The Armstrong Ranch Oak Alley Vacherie	L	Ⓓ	Alcide Dominique Box 940 Lafayette	R	24
11	PP	Pizzolato and Post Hahnville	R	⚕	Swift and Co. Box 991 Lake Charles	L	25
12	⨯W	B. K. Whitfield Box 173 Lafayette	R	4K	Chas. M. Bradford Rayne	R	26
13	＄	Mrs. Rayme Boudreau J. B. Route Cameron	R	M	Aubrey J. Marceau Box 184 Kaplan		27
14	PAT	Patrick E. Fairchild Greenwell Springs	R	−Λ−	Mrs. Agnes Tanner Box 103 Dunon	R	28

Some brands from the Louisiana Brand Book; 1955. These are modern Louisiana brands, usually with some meaning or sentiment involved in simple patterns. The letters, R and L, indicate the side on which the animal is branded.

73

Parish had become one of the main centers of Broussard habitation in the old Attakapas territory.[78] At the time, several families had moved into Calcasieu Parish, some as farmers along the lower Mermentau River, others as stockmen or graziers on the prairies. Dosité Broussard, probably a great-great grandson of *Beausoleil,* was among the Calcasieu graziers "running" 1,800 cattle in 1850.

More recently, several Broussards have been instrumental in developing the modern cattle industry in south Louisiana such as Joseph E. Broussard who founded the "Flying J" ranch at Cow Island, Vermilion Parish. Alphé Broussard, his son, developed a number of innovative techniques for raising cattle on the Cajun prairies. In the 1930's, he worked with the federal government to establish the "Bang" testing program and imported the first herd of pure-blooded Charolais cattle. Presently, the ranch is being run by Charles Broussard, the son of Alphé Broussard.

Although the Bayou Teche country formed the nucleus of the Broussard settlement in Louisiana, other parts of the colony received some Broussards during the eighteenth century. In 1769, two brothers, Firmin and Jean Broussard, were located on the east bank of the Mississippi in Ascension Parish. They were the sons of Jean Broussard and Anne Landry, who had been deported from Acadie to Maryland in 1755. It is unknown how and when these Broussards reached Louisiana, but they began a small branch of the Broussard family and remained along the Mississippi River in Ascension, Iberville and St. James parishes well into the nineteenth century.

Two other Broussard families, headed by brothers Charles and Jean, were refugees who had been exiled to France. They finally arrived in Louisiana in 1785 with 1,600 other Acadians. Charles was accompanied by his second wife, Euphrosine Marriot and four sons. Sons François and Pierre settled along the Mississippi River in West Baton Rouge Parish, where their descendants still held land in 1858. Sons Jean, Charles and Dominique settled in Lafourche and Assumption Parishes, and descendants of the latter migrated to Terrebonne Parish in 1820's. By the mid-century their line had died out or moved elsewhere. The second family from France, headed by Jean Broussard and Marguerite Comeau, had only one son, Jean-Baptiste, who by 1790 had joined other Broussards in the Attakapas area. Jean-Baptiste's progeny settled in Lafayette and Vermilion parishes.[79]

When the Acadians established their homes in Louisiana, they brought cattle raising skills with them and they were immediately aware of the rich prairie grasses and its potential as nutritious feed. Many ranchers in this area herded their cattle into the marches of Vermilion Parish during the winter to take advantage of the lush grasses. In the spring, cattle would be loaded onto barges and brought back to the ranch. The above photo, taken around 1920, shows Cajun ranchers Alphé Broussard and his future wife Odile Cade herding their cattle on Mulberry Ridge in southern Vermillion Parish.

Source: Photo courtesy of Charles Broussard

J. Maxie Broussard's political poster for his successful 1962 political campaign for the Lafayette Parish School Board. He served on the School Board from 1962 to 1978.

Finally, during the 1800's, a small line of Broussards developed in Avoyelles Parish. One Louis Broussard, possibly related to the Bayou Teche country families, first settled in the Grande Prairie area near Opelousas, but before 1795, he purchased land in Avoyelles. During the 1810's and 1820's three of his sons, Maximilien, Joseph and Jean-

The former president of La Famille Beausoleil, J. Maxie Broussard (center) shown in front of his house near Youngsville, Louisiana, in 2002, with his grandsons (l to r) Beau Broussard, Byron Luke Broussard, David Taghehchian and Matthew Taghehchian. J. Maxie Broussard died June 27, 2004.
Photo by Kermit Bouillion

Baptiste, were forming families in that area. Their descendants are likely the present-day Broussards of Avoyelles Parish.

In support of the *Congrès Mondial Acadien Louisiane 1999*, the Broussards of Louisiana incorporated (as did seventy-five other Acadian families) on December 10, 1996, as *La Famille Beausoleil Association*.[80] Its first president was Errol B. Broussard, who died tragically in an airplane accident on August 10, 1999. He was succeeded by J. Maxie Broussard, who died June 27, 2004. Other officers of the organization are: Charles Broussard, Vice-President, and Don Louis Broussard, Secretary-Treasurer.

A family reunion of the descendants of Dua Broussard and Laura Simon held at the estate of J. Maxie Broussard in May, 2002.

The City of Broussard, Louisiana, was named after Valsin Broussard, *Beausoleil's* descendant. In celebration of the *Congrès Mondial Acadien Louisiane 1999,* the City of Broussard, under the leadership of Mayor Charles Langlinais, erected a monument, designed by Maxine Duhon, to *Beausoleil* and Alexandre on July 31, 1999.[81] Brent Broussard, President of *La Famille Beausoleil Association,* and many members of the

The City of Broussard's monument to Beausoleil designed by Maxine Duhon who is pictured in the photo taken in 2004 by the author.

Broussard family contributed to the erection of the monument. The City of Broussard's promotional brochure is titled "BeauSoleil Broussard - A Driving Tour." It contains a brief history of the Broussard's contribution to the area's history.

In 1997, *La Famille Beausoleil Association,* with the support of the Jaycees of Acadiana, Inc., commissioned renowned Cajun pen and ink artist Floyd Sonnier to design a limited edition commemorative coin honoring *Beausoleil.* The coin is accompanied by the following biography:

"Sterling silver coin honors Joseph Broussard *dit Beausoleil* and his contributions to our area. From 1755 through 1758, Joseph led a small band of Acadians in a valiant effort to force the British from Acadie, present day Nova Scotia. After being imprisoned for several years, he arrived in New Orleans and was appointed Militia Captain of the

Attakapas Region, today known as Saint Martinville. Joseph Broussard *dit Beausoleil* was buried on October 20, 1765 at the camp known as *Beau Soleil* shortly after arriving in Louisiana."

Broussards, like Cajuns in general, have distinguished themselves in many fields. Those include Sheriffs Isaac Broussard, Sheriff of Lafayette

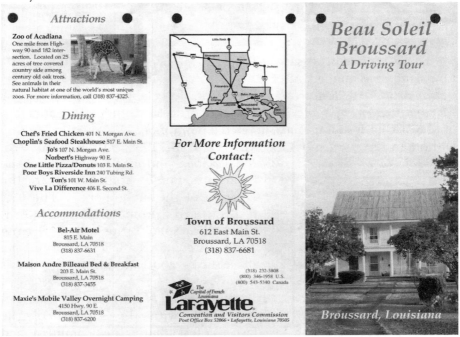

Parish (Lafayette), Theodore "T Lazair" Broussard, Sheriff of St. Martin Parish (St. Martinville) and Claude Broussard, Sheriff of Vermilion Parish (Abbeville); U.S. Senators Robert "Cousin Bob" Broussard and Edwin Broussard (New Iberia); Superintendents of Vermilion Parish School Board Lastie O. Broussard, Joseph "Joey" Hebert (Henry), and Ray Broussard (Abbeville); educators Dr. James F. Broussard,[82] L.S.U. professor (Baton Rouge), Richard Guidry, Louisiana Department of Education (Gueydan); Dr. Mark Rees, UL Lafayette archeologist (Lafayette), Dr. Doris A. Broussard Bentley, UL Lafayette (Lafayette), Steve Langlinais, UL Lafayette (Erath), R.F. and Billie Wayne Broussard (Abbeville); James P. Louviere, physics teacher (New Iberia), Connie Broussard Hebert (Henry), Numa Broussard (Erath), Teddy Broussard

(Erath), Inez LeBlanc Vincent (Erath), Harold "T-Beb" Broussard (Abbeville), Alton E. Broussard, UL Lafayette journalism professor (Lafayette); Una B. Evans (Abbeville), Nellie Broussard (Erath), Celvie Thibodeaux (Erath), Earlene Broussard, L.S.U. French professor, (Kaplan) and Dr. Vaughn Baker Simpson, former head of the UL Lafayette History Department (Lafayette).

Attorneys Lastie O. Broussard, Sr. (Abbeville), J. Weldon Granger (Houston), Catherine Mills (New Orleans), Richard Broussard (Lafayette), Hal Broussard (Lafayette), Tom Angers (Lafayette), Lavelle Broussard (Abbeville), Dwayne Broussard (Lafayette), André "Andy" Broussard (Baton Rouge), Melissa Broussard (Lafayette), Bob Broussard (Lafayette), Craig Broussard (Lafayette), Mariana Broussard (Lafayette), Troy Broussard (Lafayette), Marcus Broussard, Sr. (Abbeville), Bart Broussard (Abbeville) and Jeanne Perrin (Henry).

Artists Jay Broussard (New Iberia), Gabe Mills (Lafayette), Mary Leonise Broussard Perrin (Lafayette) and Kathy Broussard Richard (Abbeville); Presidents of the Lafayette Parish School Board J. Maxie Broussard (Lafayette) and Beverly Broussard Wilson (Lafayette); and military Colonel Sans Broussard (Maurice), Deanna Marie Brasseur, pioneering woman aviator (Ottawa, Ontario, Canada) and Brigadier General Curney J. Dronet (Erath).

Mayors Don Louis Broussard (St. Martinville), Valsin Broussard (Broussard), Robert Brady Broussard (Abbeville), Young Broussard (Abbeville), Aaron Broussard (Kenner) and Alcide "Red" Broussard (Erath); elected officials Mark Poché, President of Vermilion Parish Police Jury (Erath), Ernal Broussard (Abbeville), Paul Ed Broussard (Abbeville), Charles "CoCo" Broussard, Erath Alderman (Erath), Minos Broussard, Vermilion Parish Police Jury (Erath), Hubert Broussard, Erath Alderman (Erath), Guy Broussard (Abbeville), Paul Poché, Constable (Erath), Robert "T-Bob" Domingues, Erath Alderman (Erath), Jimmy Domingues, Vermilion Parish Registrar of Voters (Henry); Robert Vincent, Mayor Pro-Tem (Erath); Judge Marcus A. Broussard, Jr. and his son Judge Edward Broussard (Abbeville); Vermilion Parish Clerks of Court Polycarp Broussard (Abbeville), Todd Doré (Erath) and Diane Meaux Broussard (Abbeville); and Vermilion Parish assessors Daniel Broussard (Maurice), Jules Broussard (Abbeville) and Gilles Broussard (Abbeville); physicians Dr. Jerome Broussard (Lafayette), Dr. A. C. Broussard (Welsh), Dr. Emile Broussard (Abbeville), Dr. Thad

Coat of Arms

Broussard

Historiography

The Broussard Coat of Arms illustrated left was drawn by an heraldic artist from information officially recorded in an ancient herald archives. Documentation for the Broussard Coat of Arms design can be found in Rietstap Armorial General. Heraldic artists of old developed their own unique language to describe an individual Coat of Arms. In their language, the Arms (shield) is as follows:

"D'arg. a un ecusson de gu. en abime, acc. de huit grenades
d'azur, allumees du meme, rangees en orle."

When translated the blazon also describes the original colors of the Broussard Arms as it appeared centuries ago.

Family mottos are believed to have originated as battle cries in medieval times. A Motto was not recorded with this Broussard Coat of Arms.

Individual surnames originated for the purpose of more specific identification. The four primary sources for second names were: occupation, location, father's name, or personal characteristics. The surname Broussard appears to be characteristic in origin, and is believed to be associated with the French, meaning "one having disheveled hair." The supplementary sheet included with this report is designated to give you more information to further your understanding of the origin of names. Different spellings of the same original surname are a common occurrence. Dictionaries of surnames indicate probable spelling variations of Broussard to be a small fraction of the population, there are a number who have established for it a significant place in history. They include: EDWIN SIDNEY BROUSSARD (1874-1934). He started as a teacher in public schools in Louisiana and left to serve in the Spanish American War. He was elected twice to the office of District Attorney and also served two terms in the United States Senate from 1921 to 1933. NOEL MATTHIEU BROUSSARD (b. 1789). French writer on music. He published "Thiorie des sons Musicaux," in Paris in 1847, a treatise on the variability of tones according to modulation. SABASTIEN de BROUSSARD (1654-1730). French musician. His musical library (at that time) was one of the most valuable ever formed. He wrote six books on "Airs serieux et a Borre," two volumes of "Elevations et Motats," pieces for lute, violin, sonatas and chamber music. JAMES FRANCIS BROUSSARD (b. 1881). He studied at the University of Paris and received his Ph.D. at the University Montreal. He was the author of "Elements of French Pronunciation," and many other notable works in the field of linguistics.

No genealogical representation is intended or implied by this report, and it does not represent individual lineage or your family tree.

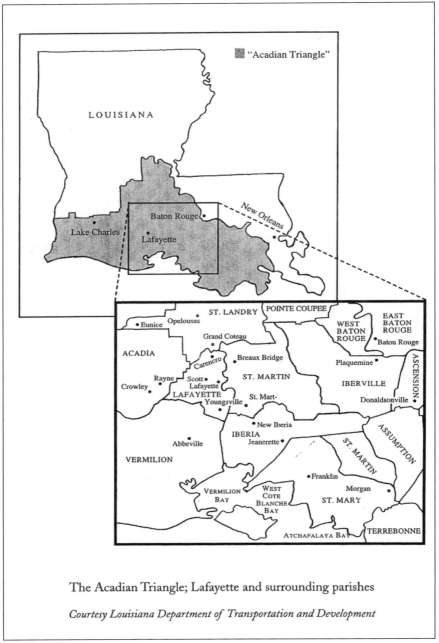

The Acadian Triangle; Lafayette and surrounding parishes

Courtesy Louisiana Department of Transportation and Development

Source: William Arceneaux, "No Spark of Malice," (Thomoson, 1999).

Broussard (Baton Rouge), Dr. Mitchell Dugas (Lafayette), Dr. Alan Broussard (Lafayette), Dr. John Thibodeaux (Erath), Dr. Bart Broussard (Lafayette) and Dr. Richard Broussard (Lafayette); and dentist Dr. Craig Landry (Lafayette).

Musicians Bonnie Broussard (Henry), accordionist Earl Broussard (Erath), singer Marc Broussard (Carencro) and his father Ted Broussard

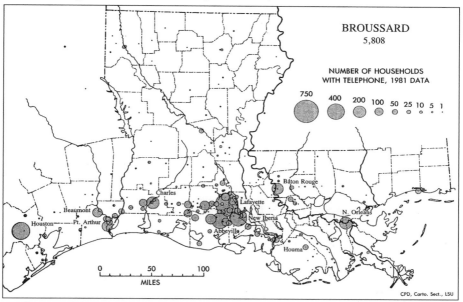

Source: Robert C. West, *An Atlas of Louisiana Surnames of French and Spanish Origin*, (Geoscience Publications, LSU).

(Lafayette), Steve Broussard (Abbeville), Stephen "Sam" Broussard, Grammy-nominated musician (Lafayette), and Natial d'Augereau, *Renaissance Cadien* (Henry); athletes Terry Perrin, National Collegiate Weightlifting Champion, UL Lafayette (New Orleans), Glenn Viltz, championship bodybuilder (Lafayette), Randall "Chip" Perrin, II, power lifter, UL Lafayette (Henry), Alley Broussard, LSU football (Lafayette), Dr. Marty Broussard, L.S.U. athletic trainer (Abbeville), Ron Guidry, New York Yankee pitcher (Carencro), Gerald Broussard, football, UL Lafayette (Lafayette), LSU Basketball Assistant Coach Rickey Broussard (Meaux), Ben Broussard, baseball (Cleveland Indians), Billy Broussard, track at UL Lafayette (Lafayette), Terrance Broussard, athletic trainer, UL Lafayette, Amy Broussard, UL Lafayette cheerleader (Erath), Keesha Broussard, UL Lafayette dance team, Phyllis Broussard,

STATE OF LOUISIANA

Council for the Development
of French in Louisiana (CODOFIL)

ETAT DE LOUISIANE

Conseil pour le Développement
du Français en Louisiane (CODOFIL)

le 29 mai 1997

Charles Langlinais
Mayor of Broussard
416 E. Railroad St.
Broussard, LA 70518

RE: *FrancoFête '99/*"Beausoleil" Broussard Project

Cher Charlie:

As President of CODOFIL, I have been organizing a statewide event which will begin January 1, 1999 to commemorate Iberville's establishing the French colony of Louisiana. We believe this statewide event will attract tourist from throughout the world to help us celebrate our French heritage and culture in Louisiana. Our preliminary plans have been well-received by agencies and municipalities. The Department of Tourism has pledged its support to the success of this event. Additionally, many Francophone countries of the world such as Luxembourg, Senegal, France, Belgium, the Maritime Provinces of Canada and Québec have assured their cooperation and support for this important event.

As part of *FrancoFête '99*, Louisiana will also host the World Acadian Congress from August 1 - 15, 1999. Lt. Gov. Kathleen Babineaux Blanco, as head of the Department of Culture, Recreation and Tourism, has pledged her support to ensure a successful tri-centennial celebration in 1999.

It has been a couple of years since we visited the idea of locating the burial site of "Beausoleil" Broussard and developing a memorial to him and his fellow Acadians. In view of the major strides made in the last few months concerning *FrancoFête '99* and the *Congrès Mondial Acadien Louisiane 1999*, I urge you to consider resurrecting this project because I believe it will be a tremendous touristic, cultural and economic benefit for your town.

As an alternative to the archeological work necessary to locate the burial site, perhaps some agreed upon site could be developed as a memorial to "Beausoleil" Broussard and his group of first Acadians to settle this region. Query: Why compromise with such a memorial? Here are some reasons: The official "Lincoln log cabin" in Illinois is actually a re-created version of the original. Also, I recently visited northern California and had the opportunity to tour the first Mexican Mission in the region. The "original Mission" was actually a re-construction of the original as a memorial to those first Mexican settlers in California.

In any event, I think that the Town of Broussard should have a committee to discuss the erection of a memorial to "Beausoleil" Broussard. I think this would be readily acceptable

217 Rue Principale Ouest, Lafayette, Louisiane 70501-6843
Tél: (318) 262-5810 • FAX: (318) 262-5812 • Gratuit: 800-259-5810

84

because in the official Canadian biography of "Beausoleil" Broussard, it is stated that he was buried near the present day town of Broussard, Louisiana. With the expected thousand of visitors coming to our state for 1999, I think that the time is proper for the development of some type of memorial.

With best wishes, I remain,

Sincèrement,

WARREN A. PERRIN
Président

WAP/dsb

cc: M. Curtis Joubert
       M. Brian Comeaux

basketball, UL Lafayette, Patrick Broussard, football, UL Lafayette, Donnie Broussard, basketball, UL Lafayette, P.D. Broussard, football, UL Lafayette, Ed "Parrain" Domingues, track, UL Lafayette (Erath), Kevin and his brother Ken Meyers, UL Baseball (Abbeville), Coach Paul Broussard (Erath), Dale Broussard, basketball, UL Lafayette (Maurice), Jimmy Poché, football, UL Lafayette, (Erath), Eric Mouton, basketball, UL Lafayette (Abbeville), Rhett Hebert, basketball, UL Lafayette, (Henry), basketball coach Ronald Broussard (Maurice), Brady Mouton, baseball, UL Lafayette (Abbeville) and Corey Broussard, basketball, UL Lafayette (Maurice); jockeys Clarence "Crépain" Broussard (Henry), Lawless Broussard (Abbeville) and Kelly Broussard (New Orleans) and professional boxer "Bad" Chad Broussard (Rayne).

Businessmen Sam Broussard (New Iberia), Justin Broussard (Abbeville), banker Roy Broussard, banker (Abbeville), Richard A. Broussard (Abbeville), banker Michael "Mickey" Broussard, Sr. (Abbeville), Michael Broussard, Jr. (Abbeville), Elwood "T-boy" Hebert, Patriot Chemical (Kenner), Bobby Broussard (Broussard), Noe R. Broussard of Broussard Brothers Inc. (Abbeville), Russell Gary (Abbeville), Claude Broussard (Abbeville), Allen Broussard (Abbeville), Michael P. Broussard (Abbeville), Jean Edmond Broussard, Jr., the founder of Bruce Foods (Broussard), David G. Broussard (Henry), photographer Ed Broussard (Lafayette), Donald Ray Dugas of Don's Boat Landing (Henry), insurance advisor Wally Broussard (L a f a y e t t e), Melanie Perrin of the U. S. Internal Revenue Service (W a s h i n g t o n , D.C.), Asa W. B r o u s s a r d (L a f a y e t t e), Mark Broussard (Abbeville), John C. Broussard (Broussard), David B. Dronet, marine

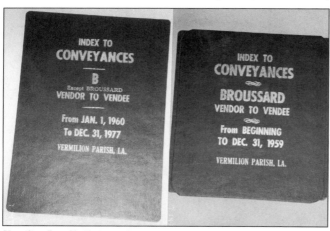

Vermilion Parish's "Index of Conveyances" requires two books for all surnames beginning with "B." These photos show the covers of index for "B except Broussard" (L) and "Broussard" (R).

transportation (Erath), Lynwood Broussard (Lafayette), Jody Dronet (Erath), banker Leo Broussard (Lafayette), Mike Landry, home designs (Lafayette), Lynn Broussard, photographer (Abbeville), Joan Marie Broussard, government budget expert (St. Lucia) and investment advisor Stan Broussard (Lafayette).

Journalists Chris Segura (Abbeville), Marcelle Bienvenu (St. Martinville), Robert Angers, Sr., founder of the *Acadiana Profile* magazine and his son Trent Angers, publisher of the *Acadiana Profile* magazine (Lafayette); architects Andrew Perrin (Austin), and James Broussard (Lafayette); and agriculture Charles Broussard, CODOFIL sponsor and cattle rancher (Abbeville), Aristide Broussard (Henry), Kern Broussard (Henry), Cleve Thibodeaux, (Erath), Ross Hebert (Henry), Eluse Dugas (Erath), Rodney Dugas (Erath), Dale Broussard, United States Department of Agriculture (Erath), Jack R. Broussard, Jr.,

The Aristide Broussard Family: (Front): Leta, Aristide, Lubria, Leontine, Rose (in Leontine's lap), and Sulie; (Back): Nolia, Aliface, Ella and Policarp. Circa 1905. Leta was the author's paternal grandmother.

Broussard Feeds (Lafayette), Alfred Baudoin (Henry) Joseph "Jo Jo" Baudoin (Abbeville), Perfay Broussard (Erath), Mark Broussard (Erath), Wilfred Langlinais (Erath), C. B. Vincent (Henry), Edier Bares (LeBlanc), Howard Broussard (Erath), Emile Thibodeaux (Abbeville); engineers, Earl Thibodeaux (Lafayette), Huey Perrin (Lafayette), Mike Guidry (Lafayette),

Theogene Broussard and Victorine Broussard, parents of Leontine Broussard, the author's paternal great-grandmother.

Allen Bares (LeBlanc) and Van Perrin (Houston).

The petroleum industry: Julien Hinckley (Henry), J.C. Broussard (Erath), Corbet Domingues (Erath), Gerald Broussard (Abbeville), Randall Perrin (Henry) and Jonas Perrin (Henry), Dennis Broussard (Erath), Oswald Broussard (Erath) and Tim Morton (Lafayette); nurses Nina Perrin (Henry), Emily Broussard Lanoix (Lafayette) and Natalie Thomas (New Orleans); Acadian Memorial co-founder Pat Resweber (St. Martinville), President Cindy D. Maraist (Lafayette), Director Brenda Comeaux Trahan (Lafayette), cultural activists Isabelle Pointer (Madison, Mississippi), Inez Gauthier (St. Martinville), radio personality Alton "Skip" Broussard (Dallas) and John Broussard, African-American Créole activist (Lafayette); the Reverends Rex Broussard (Lafayette), Richard Broussard, Henry Broussard, Warren Broussard, Paul Broussard and Monseigneur Richard Broussard; and veterinarians Dr. Sammy Thibodeaux (Erath) and George P. Broussard (New Iberia).

Today, the Broussard family is most prevalent in Vermilion Parish. This is well-documented in the Clerk of Court's conveyance records: the "B" index book's title reads *B except Broussard*, and there is a separate book listing only Broussards' transactions. Lafayette and Iberia parishes have significant concentrations of Broussards, as well as do Calcasieu, East Baton Rouge and Orleans parishes.[83] The Broussards continue to proudly call themselves Cajuns, a label that most often refers to a combination of Acadian heritage, residence in southwestern Louisiana and a general sense of difference from neighboring groups such as white Anglos, Hispanics, African-Americans and Native Americans.[84]

Emile E. Broussard and Ursule Dronet Broussard, parents of Aristide Broussard and paternal great-great grandparents of the author.

The Trahan-Broussard Saloon, Erath, Louisiana. Circa 1900. Acadian Museum archives reproduction by Kermit Bouillion.

In 1932, Nicolas "Nic" Broussard, 76 years old, went by horse and buggy from Erath, Louisiana to Washington D.C. to deliver a rooster to the President of the United States to show his support for the Democratic Party. At that time, the rooster was the symbol of the Democratic Party.

Ella Mae Broussard Perrin and Perfay Broussard, the mother and uncle of the author.

Perfay, Ella Mae (author's mother) and Effie, children of Clairville Broussard and Anatial Metrejean.

Nolia Broussard Thibodeaux, the author's great-aunt.
(Born October 2, 1892 – Died July 26, 1982)

The children of Aristide Broussard and Leontine Broussard. Seated left to right: Nolia, Policarp, Ella and Aliface. Standing left to right: Rose, Lubria, Leta (author's paternal grandmother) and Sulie.

Left to Right: Leta Broussard Perrin (author's grandmother), Henry L. Perrin (author's father), Henry M. Perrin (author's grandfather), Jonas Perrin (author's uncle) and Edez Perrin Vincent (author's aunt).

Anatial Metrejean (author's maternal grandmother) was married twice: first to Phalicia Roberts and of their marriage the following children were born: Gaston Roberts, Joseph Roberts, Ada Roberts Segura, Louvenia Roberts Guidry, Nolie Roberts Menard and Adia Roberts Gary; secondly, to Clairville Broussard of which marriage were born: Effie Broussard Bares, Perfay Broussard, and Ella Mae Broussard Perrin (author's mother).

Clairville Broussard (author's maternal grandfather) was married three times: first to Emma Menard, and the following were born: Elva Broussard, Carsaday Broussard, Elvie Broussard, Gertrude B. Gautreaux; secondly to Marie Elmire Champagne Bourgeois, of which marriage no children were born; and, thirdly to Anatial Metrejean of which marriage the following children were born: Effie Broussard Bares, Perfay Broussard and Ella Mae Broussard Perrin (author's mother).

Errol Brent Broussard, the first President of La Famille Beausoleil Assocation, *was killed in a tragic airplane accident on August 10, 1999.*

In 2002, Ella Mae Broussard Perrin, the author's mother (center), surrounded by some of her grandchildren, Rebecca Perrin Ouellet, Bruce H. Perrin and Andrew E. Perrin, the author's children.

Nicolas Jean Ouellet, born in Lafayette on March 17, 2000, son of Jean Ouellet (a native of Quebec) and Rebecca Perrin Ouellet, the author's daughter, is Beausoleil's *tenth generation descendant in Louisiana.*

Mary Leonise Broussard Perrin (daughter of Alton E. and Mary Broussard) is the wife of the author and a descendant of Beausoleil.

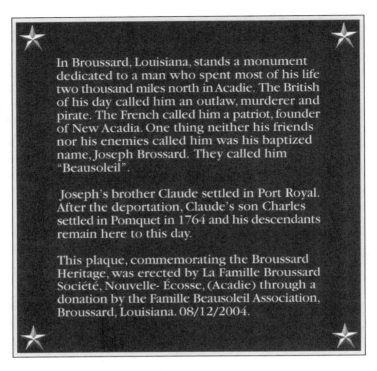

In Broussard, Louisiana, stands a monument dedicated to a man who spent most of his life two thousand miles north in Acadie. The British of his day called him an outlaw, murderer and pirate. The French called him a patriot, founder of New Acadia. One thing neither his friends nor his enemies called him was his baptized name, Joseph Brossard. They called him "Beausoleil".

Joseph's brother Claude settled in Port Royal. After the deportation, Claude's son Charles settled in Pomquet in 1764 and his descendants remain here to this day.

This plaque, commemorating the Broussard Heritage, was erected by La Famille Broussard Société, Nouvelle- Écosse, (Acadie) through a donation by the Famille Beausoleil Association, Broussard, Louisiana. 08/12/2004.

In 2004, Sheila Broussard, President of the Broussard Family Reunion during the Congrès Mondial Acadien 2004, is shown admiring the Broussard Memorial in Pomquet, Nova Scotia.

On August 9, 2004, during "Cajuns Come Home to Grand Pré" celebration of the Congrès Mondial Acadien 2004, *the author is shown with the Queen's Royal Proclamation which is on display in the church at Grand-Pré Historic Site in Grand Pré, Nova Scotia. Photo by Kermit Bouillion.*

On August 11, 2004 during the Broussard Family Reunion in Pomquet, Nova Scotia, Charles Broussard, Vice-President of La Famille Beausoleil Association *of Louisiana, is shown presenting the 2004 "*Beausoleil Award*" to the author. Photo by Kermit Bouillion.*

PART II
REDEMPTION: THE PETITION TO OBTAIN AN APOLOGY FOR THE ACADIAN DEPORTATION

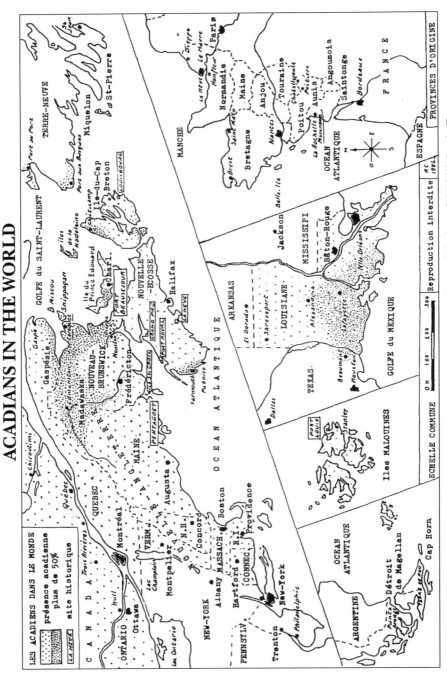

Map, courtesy of *Les Amitiés acadiennes*, 2 rue Ferdinand-Babre, 705015 Paris France.

CHAPTER 10
SKETCHES OF AN ACADIAN JOURNEY

On July 28, 1755, the order of exile was signed. On September 5, 1755, a tragic day in Acadian history, 418 Acadian men and teenage boys at Grand Pré were ensnared and told the following by Col. John Winslow:

> I have received from his Excellency Governor Lawrence, the King's Commission which I have in my hand and by whose orders you are convened together to manifest to you his Majesty's final resolution to the French inhabitants of this his Province of Nova Scotia who for almost half a century have had more indulgence granted them, than any of his subjects in any part of his Dominions ... That your lands and tenements, cattle of all kinds and livestock of all sorts are forfeited to the Crown with all other your effects saving your money and household goods and you yourselves to be removed from this his province.

Simply because the Acadian delegates refused to sign another oath of allegiance that would have stripped them of their rights, the British Crown made the decision to deport them and to confiscate their belongings. The Acadians had done no wrong. With the possible exception of a few men following the French Abbé Le Loutre, they had not given any sign of insurrection. All they had done was continue to speak French, practice Catholicism and turn lands no one else wanted into the envy of the British Empire.

In spite of any criticism one may have about the present day Petition for an apology - all those involved are long dead, another example of political correctness run amok, what difference does it make, etc. - there are a few incontrovertible facts that made it necessary: on July 28, 1755, France and England were at peace. Furthermore, the Acadians, by virtue of the Treaty of Utrecht of 1713, were British, not French, subjects. They had already pledged allegiance to the British Crown with certain stipulations, such as not being required to take up arms against the French. Under the rule of law, these are paramount distinctions.

The *Grand Dérangement* set into motion a series of events that have repercussions to this day. There are economists who opine that Nova Scotia's economy was devastated for generations after the expulsion of the farmers who knew how to work the land, and indeed the ill effects are still felt today, if to a lesser degree.

The main benefit of the Royal Proclamation is to remind people that this sort of atrocity can happen at any time to anyone. It is submitted that because *Beausoleil* led the Acadian resistance, the Royal Proclamation grants to him, as representative of the Acadian people, a posthumous redemption. It reads:

> Whereas the Acadian people, through the vitality of their community, have made a remarkable contribution to Canadian society for almost 400 years; ...
> Whereas on July 28, 1755, the Crown, in the course of administering the affairs of the British colony of Nova Scotia, made the decision to deport the Acadian people; ... And whereas, by Order in Council P.C. 2003 1967 of December 6, 2003, the Governor in Council has directed that a proclamation do issue designating July 28 of every year as A Day of Commemoration of the Great Upheaval, commencing on July 28, 2005; Now know you that we, by and with the advice of Our Privy Council for Canada, do by this Our Proclamation, effective on September 5, 2004, designate July 28 of every year as A Day of Commemoration of the Great Upheaval commencing on July 28, 2005.

In 1990, the Petition was commenced to officially declare an end of the Acadian exile because it was carried out in violation of British and international law; therefore the British government and Crown had a moral obligation to acknowledge that a wrong occurred: the Acadians should not have been exiled as criminals. Richard Baudoin penned the first article written about the Petition in *The Times of Acadiana*, ("Time to End the Exile," Volume 10, Number 23, February 14, 1990, pages 8-11), it begins as follows:

> The exile begins never to end ... Warren Perrin is haunted by this line from Longfellow's poem Evangeline. It conveys the tragedy of the Acadian people, banished from their ancestral lands by a violent and cruel governor bent on genocide. It describes

an injustice that has never been acknowledged, a crime never punished, a wrong never righted.

Perrin, an Acadian by origin ('90 percent' Broussard on his paternal and maternal sides) and an attorney by profession, is seeking to close the book on this gross violation of basic human rights. He has drafted a lawsuit that sets out the grievances of the Acadian people and asks for compensation from the government of Great Britain, in whose name the deed was carried out 235 years ago.

Perrin does not seek monetary damages, either for the lands that were seized from his ancestors in Acadie nor for the suffering they endured during their odyssey from Nova Scotia to South Louisiana. Rather he wants the English to admit that *Le Grand Dérangement* ('the clearest case of genocide you can find') was carried out in violation of English and international law of the time. And he wants the British government to erect a monument – *une symbole physique* – which would represent the end of the exile.

Five years later, Bernard Chaillot wrote an article for *The Daily Iberian,* "Erath Man Seeks Formal Apology for Acadian Exile," July 3, 1995:

Warren Perrin said he is on a mission to help right a grievous wrong – the genocide and scattering of an oppressed minority group in eastern Canada more than 200 years ago. An attorney, founder of an Acadian museum here and president of the Council for the Development of French in Louisiana, Perrin said he is seeking a formal apology from the British government for the expulsion of Acadians from Nova Scotia in the mid-eighteenth century. Perrin also said the deportation order, which exiled French Acadian settlers from their homes and separated families and forced many to undertake risky sea voyages to start new lives in Louisiana and elsewhere, never was annulled.

This is how the *Times of Acadiana* ("Good - All Apologies," Vol. 24, No. 13, December 17, 2003) reported the signing of the Royal

Proclamation:

> Understatement: Warren Perrin is extremely delighted. At 2 p.m. Wednesday, December 9, Governor General Adrienne Clarkson, the Canadian head of state and the Queen of England's representative in Canada, signed a royal proclamation that not only acknowledged the expulsion of some 15,000 Acadians from Canada but recognized the wrongs it caused. The proclamation - signed in Ottawa - also designated July 28 as an official day to commemorate the Acadians and the expulsion. Perrin started the movement for recognition and apology in 1990 by sending a letter to Queen Elizabeth II and her current prime minister. Perrin, who even declined offers of money for endowed scholarships to quiet his actions, credits the non-confrontational and non-financial nature of the request for its success. Whether or not talk of the queen reading the proclamation at Grand Pré, National Historic Site in Nova Scotia, during a royal visit slotted for 2005 is true doesn't seem to matter to Perrin. 'We are never going to forget it, but it's closure. The queen is finally saying what happened to you was wrong and it was in my name. She doesn't say I am terribly sorry, but there are many ways to apologize.'

Therefore, instead of a proposed monument acknowledging the responsibility of the British Crown in the events of 1755 as had originally requested, there is now a national holiday. Instead of the many, but limited, number of visitors to a commemorative site learning about this tragedy, now tens of millions of people will learn about it, thus adding to the hopes of all people that such a thing never happens again.

CHAPTER 11
THE PETITION

The Petition represented Acadians seeking redress against the British government and the Queen as representative of the British Crown. The Petition was delivered on January 5, 1990, to then British Prime Minister Margaret Thatcher and the Queen of England, wherein six issues were set forth therein as follows:

1. Restoration of the status of "French neutrals."
2. An inquiry into the deportation by a fair panel.
3. Officially ending the Acadian exile by a declaration annulling the Order of Deportation.
4. An acknowledgment that tragedies occurred.
5. An acknowledgment that the action occurred contrary to existing international and/or English law.
6. A symbolic gesture of good will by the erection of a monument to memorialize the "end of the exile."

The Petition was not filed in a court of law; it sought no compensation for the Acadians. Within thirty days of receiving the Petition, the British government and Crown retained the Houston law firm of Bracewell and Patterson to represent its interest. Negotiations commenced shortly thereafter; they ultimately proved to be successful.

The Petition contained the same six issues that were presented once before to the King of England in 1760 by the Acadians exiled to Pennsylvania. Four Acadians who spoke English fluently traveled to London to deliver their petition to King George II. However, the messengers were received contemptuously. The King refused to have it read or considered.[85] Therefore, the Petition filed in 1990 was actually an amending Petition which, by law, related back to the original date of filing, that of 1760.

Looking over the history of civilization, it can be seen that one of the most difficult things for human beings to do has been to remain loyal to human decency. In the comfort of one's own home it is easy to take a stand against brutality and the deprivation of liberty. Ask anyone if they condone these things, and the answer would be no; but the ugly fact is that they often do. Most often injustice is committed when persons are seduced by a cause or an ideology.

Once it is believed that a group of people is the cause of a problem, it often logically follows that the solution to that problem is to eliminate the group. The expulsion of the Acadians was an ethnic cleansing. Lawrence's paranoia over the Acadians' presence, coupled with the Crown's desire for further colonial expansion, did not justify a series of actions so drastic that they could only be called ethnic cleansing.

The main issues of the petition were as follows:

A. The Exile Began During a Time of Peace:

On September 1, 1755, during a time of peace, Lawrence sent out instructions to his troops: all Acadian lands, tenements, cattle and livestock were to be forfeited with all other effects. All French inhabitants of Nova Scotia were to be removed. A trap was then set: all Acadian citizens were ordered to assemble in their churches[86] to hear an important proclamation by the English government. However, upon their arrival, the doors and windows were barred and they were made prisoners and ordered to await the arrival of ships. They were then forced onto overcrowded ships without sufficient provisions, and sent to an unfriendly land: the thirteen Anglo-American Colonies.

Although there were initial skirmishes between the French and the British as early as May of 1754, prior to the Seven Years' War in the Ohio River Valley, the official declaration of war did not take place until May 18, 1756, long after the Acadian's exile had begun. Accordingly, under international law, it was not legal to confiscate the property of these Acadians as it might have been during a time of war. Prior to the official declaration of war, the rights of these subjects should have been honored.

B. There was No Law Providing for the Penalty Inflicted:

Even if we are to assume that some of the Acadians engaged in political crimes and acts of treason, under neither English nor international law were there provisions for the confiscation of the properties of a father of a family, or the punishment of his wife and

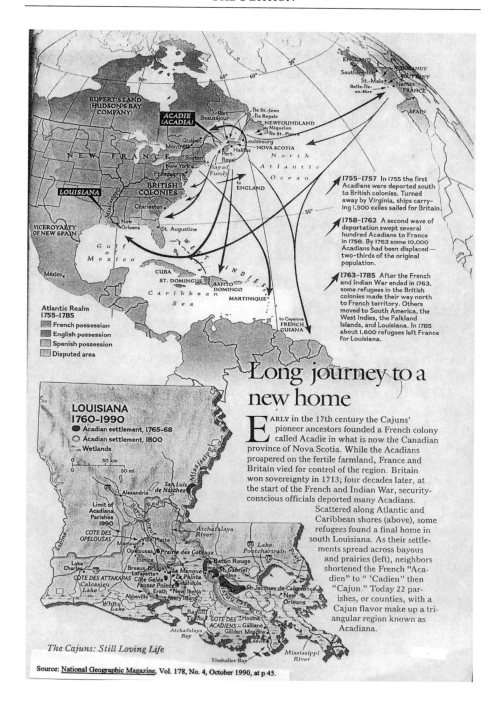

1755–1757 In 1755 the first Acadians were deported south to British colonies. Turned away by Virginia, ships carrying 1,500 exiles sailed for Britain.

1758–1762 A second wave of deportation swept several hundred Acadians to France in 1758. By 1763 some 10,000 Acadians had been displaced — two-thirds of the original population.

1763–1785 After the French and Indian War ended in 1763, some refugees in the British colonies made their way north to French territory. Others moved to South America, the West Indies, the Falkland Islands, and Louisiana. In 1785 about 1,600 refugees left France for Louisiana.

Atlantic Realm
1755–1785

- French possession
- English possession
- Spanish possession
- Disputed area

LOUISIANA
1760–1990

- Acadian settlement, 1765–68
- Acadian settlement, 1800
- Wetlands

Long journey to a new home

EARLY in the 17th century the Cajuns' pioneer ancestors founded a French colony called Acadie in what is now the Canadian province of Nova Scotia. While the Acadians prospered on the fertile farmland, France and Britain vied for control of the region. Britain won sovereignty in 1713; four decades later, at the start of the French and Indian War, security-conscious officials deported many Acadians.

Scattered along Atlantic and Caribbean shores (above), some refugees found a final home in south Louisiana. As their settlements spread across bayous and prairies (left), neighbors shortened the French "Acadien" to " 'Cadien" then "Cajun." Today 22 parishes, or counties, with a Cajun flavor make up a triangular region known as Acadiana.

The Cajuns: Still Loving Life

Source: <u>National Geographic Magazine</u>, Vol. 178, No. 4, October 1990, at p 45.

107

children, for an offense that might have been committed by the father. Although the law provided severe sanctions for political crimes, there were no provisions for the confiscation of lands or any other possessions of a group of persons and their banishment for any reason whatsoever.[87] As a consequence of the Treaty of Utrecht and Queen Anne's Edict, the Acadians had a right to abide in their lands and not be driven from them unless by the sentence of the law.[88]

C. Royal Prerogative Was Ignored by Lawrence:

Queen Anne's Edict expanded upon the rights of the Acadians pursuant to the Treaty of Utrecht. Her pronunciation was Royal Prerogative, which could not be ignored or overruled by a government official. The refusal to comply with Queen Anne's orders, which had allowed the Acadians to keep their lands and enjoy them without any obstacle or hindrance as fully and freely as the other British subjects did on their land, must be viewed as an abuse of power by Lawrence and a violation of basic British law existing at that time.[89]

D. Lieutenant-Governor Lawrence Lacked the Authority to Act:

At the time of the exile, Peregrine Hopson was governor. He left for England due to illness in November of 1753. Colonel Charles Lawrence, who had been in the colony since 1741, and who had become a member of the Advisory Council of the governor, was soon elevated and appointed Lieutenant-Governor. Shortly thereafter, he illegally changed governor Hopson's orders. He was subsequently named Governor on December 24, 1755, but under English law, Lieutenant-Governor Lawrence had no authority to change the policies which had been in effect since 1713. Lieutenant-Governor Lawrence, acting without direct authorization from superiors and contrary to existing British law, ordered unmerciful punishment for all the Acadians, treating them as rebels and criminals.

Why were the Acadians so feared even after they had been deprived of their arms and boats? The French had been expelled from all their strongholds on the coast. The argument that there was a threat posed by the Acadians is belied by the fact that the relation of the population was some two hundred British to one Acadian, and these Acadians had remained neutral even in time of war. Their neutrality was tested in time of war and not found wanting. The irony is that the Acadians were deported in a time of peace. Since the Acadians occupied all of the good farming lands in Nova Scotia, and their deportation made these lands available for the New England and Halifax colonists, it was merely a sham for Lawrence to claim that the Acadians posed a security risk to British interests in North America.

E. Precedents - It Is Never Too Late To "Right A Wrong":

Most countries with colonialist histories have to wrench themselves into gazing into the deeper, darker chasms of their past: Americans with slavery and the near-genocide of the indigenous peoples; the Spaniards and Italians with fratricidal war and fascism; the French collaboration with the Nazis during World War II; Germans with the Holocaust.

Initial public reaction to the Petition was mixed. There was universal acceptance in Louisiana, even among non-Cajuns, and other Francophone countries. However, the reaction was mixed in Canada, especially among Acadians. Most Canadian Anglophones viewed the Petition as an attempt to embarrass their Queen and poke fun at the whole concept of royalty. Much more publicity was generated in Canada where the battle over Quebec's sovereignty raged on during the 1990's. Eventually, the Petition gained acceptance and received the support of Acadians throughout the world - especially fueled by the interest in the first two *Congrès Mondiaux Acadiens.*

ÉDITORIAL

Source: *Le Devoir*, May 10, 2001.

Translation: "Apologies?! It's them who should thank us for having deported them to a warm country where the taxes are lower."

Newspaper: "Deportation of the Acadians: Waiting 250 Years for an Apology."

CHAPTER 12
APOLOGIES

R ather than use a confrontational approach to achieve the goals of the Petition, it was decided early on to convince the British that their acknowledgment of the wrongs done to the Acadians would be viewed by historians as an apology that was long overdue and well-deserved. The effort was aided by a decade of peace among the world's powers and a period of introspection by many nations, the result being that many apologized for their historical misdeeds.

The British government publicly stated that it was too late to raise these issues. The following was submitted in opposition to that argument: In 1760, Acadians filed a petition; therefore, the amending Petition filed in 1990 related back to the initial filing because the issues raised in the initial Petition were never addressed, much less resolved. Further, the Order of Deportation that was signed on July 28, 1755, was still in effect to this day, and therefore was a contemporary issue that could be raised presently because it was an ongoing violation of Acadians' rights. The parties responsible in 1755 (government and Crown) still existed as viable entitles today, and are therefore answerable for the wrongs committed in the past.

Some examples germane to the issues that were raised by the petition:

a. In 1988, Japanese-Americans obtained reparations and an apology from the United States government for the unspeakable treatment they received during World War II.
b. In 1990, Canada apologized to Canadian-Italians for the unspeakable treatment they received during World War II.
c. In December, 1991, North and South Korea signed a Treaty of Reconciliation ending the Korean War 28 years after the hostilities ceased.
d. In January, 1992, Japan offered an apology for forcing tens of thousands of Korean women to serve as prostitutes during World War II.
e. In March, 1998, U.S. President Clinton apologized to

Source: *Concour De Plaidoiries,* Normandy, France, 1993.

Translation: "We could send them to St. Helena!"
"But they are Acadians sir, not Corsicans."

Source: *Concour De Plaidoiries,* Normandy, France, 1993.

Translation: "Sorry counselor but during that period in history I was not Prime Minister to Her Gracious Majesty."

descendants of Africans who were victims of slavery, and in October, 1992, to native Hawaiians for the U.S. government's involvement in the overthrow of their island kingdom in 1893.

f.   On July 15, 1998, during the re-burial of Czar Nicholas II, President Yeltsin of Russia apologized to the Russian people for the eighty years of the "sins of communism".

Some examples of apologies by Britain follow:

a.   In October, 1992, Queen Elizabeth II issued an apology and sought reconciliation with the citizens of Dresden, Germany, for the World War II firebombing of the city (as an appeasement by Churchill to Stalin) by an insubordinate British Commander, Sir Arthur "Bomber" Harris. (Note: the event occurred 56 years ago).

b.   In June, 1995, Queen Elizabeth II personally signed a document of reconciliation and personally apologized to the Maori people of New Zealand for taking their island from their ancestors in the mid-1800's. (Note: the event occurred approximately 150 years ago.)

c.   In October, 1997, Prime Minister Tony Blair issued an apology to the Irish people for the British government's actions during the Irish "potato famine" in the early 1800's. (Note: the event occurred approximately 150 years ago.)

d.   In October, 1997, Queen Elizabeth II symbolically apologized to the Indian people for the killing of 379 civilians by British forces in 1919 in the city of Amritsar, India. (Note: the event occurred approximately 80 years ago.)

e.   On January 30, 1998, after years of Catholic demands, Prime Minister Tony Blair announced a new judicial inquiry into "Bloody Sunday," the January 30, 1972 killing of 13 Catholic protesters by British soldiers in Northern Ireland. (Note: the event occurred 26 years ago.)

f.   On April 3, 1998, Britain apologized to Israelis for the confiscation of Jewish bank accounts and withholding of those funds since World War II. (Note: the event occurred 55 years ago).

Finally, and significantly, in 1951, Britain sought and obtained an apology from Japan on behalf of the British soldiers who suffered mistreatment while held captive by the Japanese during World War II. Significantly, this shows that the British demanded and received an acknowledgment for the wrongs done to their own people during a time of war.

Securing a repudiation of the exile helps to put the tragedy to rest, much as the family of a murder victim seeks to relieve its suffering by seeing the murderer express an act of contrition for the crime. History, as it now stands, incorrectly judged the Acadians as a corrupt people who refused to cooperate and honor their oath. The reconciliation should restore the good name of the Acadian people. National contrition teaches an important lesson to all and thus helps prevent future horrors.[90]

CHAPTER 13
SUPPORT FOR THE PETITION

The Petition received support from throughout the world. Presentations on it were made at many international events including the 1993 World Human Rights Conference in Caen, France, the *Congrès Mondial Acadien 1994* in New Brunswick, Canada and the *Convention de l'Association des Jurists d'Expression Française du Canada* on June 14, 1993. In a letter dated September 7, 1993, Damien R. Leader, *Chargé d'Affaires* of the Embassy of the United States to the Holy See, Rome, Italy, expressed official support for the Petition: "Your efforts to obtain a declaration of the end of the Acadian Exile are commendable." Moreover, the Louisiana Legislature unanimously approved the Petition in an official resolution in 1993, pursuant to Senate Concurrent Resolution Number 159 and signed by the President of the Senate and Speaker of the House of Representatives. In June, 1994, by order of the Senate President, the resolution requesting the apology was personally hand-delivered by Ann Johnson, Director of Administrative Services Division, Louisiana Senate, to the Prime Minister of England and Mark R. Turner, Desk Officer, North American Department, London, England.

During the *Congrès Mondial Acadien Louisiane 1999,* a Mock Trial was sponsored by the Ninth Annual Judge Allen M. Babineaux Comparative International Law Symposium. The event was sponsored by the American Bar Association, Louisiana Bar Association and Lafayette Parish Bar Association. An overflow crowd of people attended the trial, which was held in U. S. Federal District Court on August 13, 1999, in Lafayette before a panel of Louisiana judges representing the Louisiana Supreme Court, Third Circuit Court of Appeal and district judges. After hearing arguments concerning various issues raised in the Petition, the 15-judge panel unanimously ruled that the Petition should proceed to conclusion. On August 13, 1999, the headline story in the *Daily Advertiser* newspaper in Lafayette read: "The Queen on Trial." [91]

Other supportive developments for the Petition included public debates, lectures, resolutions, interviews, honors, documentaries, editorials, legal publications and articles in Louisiana, the United States, France, Belgium, Canada, England, Australia, Vietnam, Germany,

Switzerland, Luxembourg, Senegal, Romania and Italy. An article in the *National Geographic Magazine* published in 1990 stated:

> In a perfect illustration of Cajun moderation, a Lafayette lawyer named Warren Perrin recently petitioned the Queen of England to bring an official end to the Acadian exile by admitting that it was a violation of English and international law. 'I wanted to do this,' he told me, 'so when my children ask why their ancestors came here, I don't have to say they were "criminals." It's never too late to correct a wrong.' [92]

Much support in Canada resulted from the endorsement of the Petition by Howard Crosby, member of the Canadian Parliament representing Nova Scotia, the members of the Francophone section of the New Brunswick Bar Association and Senator Gerard Comeau, representative of Nova Scotia in the Parliament. National support was engendered by an article in the *Los Angeles Times Magazine* written by Eric Lawlor, who solicited the British government for a quote:

> 'I don't think the government feels there's any particular point in having an official investigation or anything like that,' says Helen Mann, Britain's vice consul in Houston. 'And I don't see how you could possibly describe a contemporary Cajun as living in exile. To say that a Cajun who travels to Nova Scotia is breaking the law is a real stretch.' [93]

The article also discussed, for the first time, the reason the Petition was begun. The reference to "one of his sons" is to Bruce Perrin:

> Perrin's life has changed dramatically in the last five years. And all because of a question posed by one of his sons. 'Why were the Cajuns thrown out of Nova Scotia?' the boy wanted to know. 'What did we do wrong?'

In 1995, Louise McKinney wrote "Perrin's Petition" for *The World and I* magazine, and again mentioned the genesis of the Petition and its relation to *Beausoleil*:

Perrin smiles, remembering the time when, seated with his then-six-year-old son, Bruce, he first related the story of Joseph *Beausoleil* Broussard. 'You mean, our ancestors were criminals?' asked Bruce brightly.[94]

In the same article, Ms. McKinney discussed the entire history of the Petition and its relationship to the Broussard ancestry:

Warren Perrin, husband to Mary Perrin (née Broussard), son of Ella Mae Broussard Perrin – who is, in turn, sister of Effie and Perfay Broussard, the children of Clairville and Anatial (née Metrejean) Broussard. Clairville Broussard is a direct descendant of Joseph *'Beausoleil'* Broussard, the legendary resistance fighter who, in 1765, was one of the first Acadians to arrive in New Orleans. He was attracted to the area by the prospect of land grants overseen by the Spanish governor, Antonio de Ulloa.

It is estimated that between 1990 and 2003 there were about 300 articles written about the Petition. The one which rallied more support to the cause than any other was an article by *The Economist* magazine. Some quotes follow:

Many Cajuns, including Mr. Perrin, still speak an exotic version of French, but now their difference is appreciated. Cajun music and Cajun cooking have won admirers around the world. Cajun intellectuals at the University of South Louisiana in Lafayette say that an apology from the British, however belated, would right an injustice. Britain's Foreign Office replies with raised eyebrows, that today's Britain cannot be held responsible for something done 250 years ago.

Perrin's decision to sue Britain is based on America's apology to Japanese-Americans for their treatment during the second world war. He discovered not only that Britain had never apologized but that Acadians are still formally regarded as traitors and, in theory, still face the death penalty if they return to Nova Scotia. He believes he has a solid legal case. The deportation of 1755

117

was done in peacetime, and the victims were British subjects. Perrin believes the British crown still remains liable for what happened, under the principle of *respondeat superior.*" [95]

Importantly, the *Economist*'s article also mentioned the support which came from attendance of the World Francophone Summit in Hanoi, Vietnam in 1999:

> That led to an invitation from President Jacques Chirac to attend the recent meeting of French-speaking countries in Vietnam. On the French presidential aircraft Mr. Perrin found Mr. Chirac towering over him and exclaiming, hand on heart, '*Ah, oui, Louisiane! Trés chaleureuse!*' (rough translation: `Ah yes, Louisiana! Very welcoming'). Mr. Chirac told Mr. Perrin he had spent several happy months as a young man in New Orleans, looking into the economics of the city's port.

In summary, because of the tremendous interest shown by the local, state, national and international media the press played a major role in securing a successful conclusion to the Petition. Hopefully, future generations will view the Petition as an example of how people, who were victims of governmental oppression, can obtain redemption without resorting to violence. As the then Secretary-General of the United Nations Boutros-Boutros Ghali said during his address for the opening of the first *Congrès Mondial Acadien 1994,* "the world should look to the Acadian experience to see how disputes among people can be resolved peacefully." Since the September 11, 2001, terrorist attacks in the United States, this seems to be more important than ever.

CHAPTER 14
THE ROYAL PROCLAMATION

The ramifications of the Royal Proclamation are two-fold: the symbolic establishment of a reconciliation between the former imperial occupying force, the British, with that of the occupied people, the Acadians. For the Acadian people, this presents an opportunity to finally be on a par with the former colonial power. Secondly, the Royal Proclamation sets the standard for what is morally right in the twenty-first century for governments still engaged in cultural and political imperialism throughout the world.

During the *Grand Dérangement* the military force used by the British changed the balance of power which in turn generated an enormous amount of stress upon a normally peaceful people. *Beausoliel's* militant actions may be better understood as a reaction to this extraordinary stress imposed upon by the Acadians by the British military forces. Like other revolutionary figures, such as Ernesto "Che" Guevara, Toussaint L'Ouverture, Gerry Adams and Thomas Jefferson, *Beausoleil* fought against an imperial power by using the strategy of "by any means necessary." After nearly 250 years, *Beausoleil's* efforts to resist assimilation into the British culture have finally achieved symbolic redemption. Despite constant external pressures to assimilate, Acadians still maintain their separate cultural identity. This achievement was inspired by the efforts of *Beausoleil*, the Acadian revolutionary, and the Crown has finally acknowledged this fact with the Royal Proclamation.

In January of 1990, a copy of the Petition seeking an apology for the Acadian deportation was delivered to the representative of the British Crown, Queen Elizabeth II.

On December 9, 2003, Queen Elizabeth II symbolically apologized to the Acadians. An apology is defined as "an expression of regret." It may take many forms, including words or symbolic acts. One can apologize for one's own misdeeds or for the misdeeds of a group of which one is a member. In order to be credible, one has to have the authority and capacity to make that apology. For example, the Pope apologized for past episodes of Christian anti-Semitism.

The Royal Proclamation of December 9, 2003, was signed by Adrienne Clarkson, the governor-general of Canada and official

Royal proclamation on deportation

To All Whom These Presents shall come or in whom the same may in any way concern, Greeting:

A Proclamation

Whereas the Acadian people, through the vitality of their community, have made a remarkable contribution to Canadian society for almost 400 years;

Whereas on July 28, 1755, the Crown, in the course of administering the affairs of the British colony of Nova Scotia, made the decision to deport the Acadian people;

Whereas the deportation of the Acadian people, commonly known as the Great Upheaval, continued until 1763 and had tragic consequences, including the deaths of many thousands of Acadians from disease, in shipwrecks, in their places of refuge and in prison camps in Nova Scotia and England as well as in the British colonies in America;

Whereas We acknowledge these historical facts and the trials and suffering experienced by Acadian people during the Great Upheaval;

Whereas We hope that the Acadian people can turn the page on this dark chapter of their history;

Whereas Canada is no longer a British colony but a soveriegn state, by and under the Constitution of Canada;

Whereas when Canada became a soverign state, with regard to Canada, the Crown in right of Canada and of the provinces succeeded to the powers and prerogatives of the Crown in right of the United Kingdom;

Whereas we, in Our role as Queen of Canada exercise the executive power by and under the Constitution of Canada;

Whereas this Our present Proclamation does not, under any circumstances, constitute a recognition of legal or financial responsibility by the Crown in right of Canada and of the provinces and is not, under any circumstances, a recognition of, and does not have any effect upon, any right or obligation of any person or group of persons;

And whereas, by Order in Council P.C. 2003 1967 of December 6, 2003, the Governor in Council has directed that a proclamation do issue designating July 28 of every year as "A Day of Commemoration of the Great Upheaval", commenciing on July 28, 2005;

Now know you that we, by and with the advice of Our Privy Council for Canada, do by this Our Proclamation, effective on Sepetember 5, 2004, designate July 28 of every year as "A Day of Commemoration of the Great Upheaval commencing on July 28, 2005.

Of all which, our Loving Subjects and all others whom these Presents may concern are hereby required to take notice and govern themselves accordingly.

In testimony whereof, We have cause this Our Proclamation to be published and the Great Seal of Canada be hereunto affixed.

Witness:
Our Right Trusty and Well beloved Adrienne Clarkson, Chancellor and Principal Companion of Our Order of Canada, Chancellor and Commander of Our Order of Military Merit, Chancellor and Commander of Our Order of Merit of the Police Forces, Governor General and Commander in Chief of Canada. At Our Government House, in Our City of Ottawa, this ninth day of December in the year of Our Lord two thousand and three and in the fifty second year of Our reign.

representative of Queen Elizabeth II, who embodies the British Crown. The Royal Proclamation is a clear repudiation of the wrongs committed during the Acadian deportation in the name of the British Crown by the hegemonic colonial British authorities.

According to Donna Doucet of the *Société Promotion Grand-Pré*, the society has invited Queen Elizabeth II to visit Grand Pré next summer for the 250th anniversary of the Acadian deportation. It is hoped that on July 28, 2005, the first observance of the "Day of Commemoration of the Great Upheaval" as designated in the Royal Proclamation, Queen Elizabeth II will read her Royal Proclamation, which is now on display in the *Saint-Charles-aux-mines* church at Grand-Pré National Historic Site of Canada. The only certified copy of the Queen's Royal Proclamation in Louisiana is on display in a permanent exhibit at the Acadian Museum of Erath. The exhibit also contains the original Petition, as well as supporting documents, research materials, letters and articles published on the subject.

On August 9, 2001, the effort to obtain the Royal Proclamation was aided by merging the efforts of the Petition with those of the *Société Nationale de l'Acadie* under the leadership of its then-President Euclide Chaisson, who was able to unite all of the Acadian organizations of the world behind the effort and rally the support of Canadian Prime Minister Jean Chretien and the Canadian government. Today, the organization is headed by Michel Cyr, attorney from Moncton, New Brunswick.

The Royal Proclamation was praised by newspaper articles in Louisiana,[96] France,[97] Canada,[98] and the United States,[99] novels,[100] newsletters,[101] television and radio programs,[102] magazine articles[103] and editorials.[104] The Petition will hopefully be a rallying point for a continued cultural revitalization long into the twenty-first century. Achieving the Petition's goals will provide the Acadian people their long overdue redemption. For over one hundred and fifty years, the symbol of the Acadian people has been Evangeline, an imaginary archetypal Acadian character created by the American poet, Henry Wadsworth Longfellow, in his classic poem *Evangeline*. Her memory is embodied in an oak tree, a statue and other monuments throughout the world, however, the story of *Evangeline* has no factual basis; it is even held in contempt and ridiculed by some members of the Acadian population.[105] Thus, our only shrine was based on a myth. It was respectfully submitted that there was a need for a tangible symbol of the Acadians' history which all Acadians could respect. The Royal Proclamation established July 28th of each year as a day commemorating the sufferings of the Acadians during the deportation. Although not a physical symbol, the day of remembrance will be a wonderful opportunity for all people to honor the memory of the Acadians who endured so much unnecessary suffering.

The general impression one has of the deportation and the Acadians' years of exile is of the misery and distress. Colonel Winslow's diary entry of October 8, 1755, reads:

> Began to embark the inhabitants who went off very solitarily and unwillingly, the women in great distress carrying off their children in their arms, others carrying their decrepit parents in their carts and all their goods moving in great confusion and it appeared a scene of woe and distress.[106]

Winslow's words are vivid; he is accurately reporting a scene of human suffering. But, these words are utterly inadequate as a summary of Acadian reaction to what occurred. After all, the Acadian culture *survived* deportation and exile.[107]

Injustice is not a phenomenon that occurred only in the past. It happens today: the leftist will justify leftist indecency; the rightist, rightist indecency; the nationalist, nationalist indecency; the religious, religious indecency. One can see evidence of similar deplorable action today. In April, 2004, the world marked ten years since the 1994 slaughter that killed at least 500,000 in Rwanda. On July 10, 2004, United Nations' Secretary-General Kofi Annan warned that a new genocide was unfolding in Sudan where the government - an Arab state - appeared to have little inclination to do much for the mostly black African tribesmen under attack. The latest ethnic slaughter was described thusly:

> They shot him in his house. They blew her apart with a bomb. They cut him to pieces with swords. They dragged her into the desert and raped her. As the world's attention was turned to crises in the Middle East, a slaughter has raged for 17 months in Sudan's Darfur region. Arab gunmen on horses and camels, backed by bombers and helicopter gunships, have razed

hundreds of black African villages, killed tens of thousands and driven more than 1 million from their homes. 'They say they don't want to see black skin on this land again,' said Issa Bushara, whose brother and cousin were gunned down.[108]

Great Britain has chosen to take the moral high ground in electing to acknowledge that wrongs were committed in its name during the Acadian deportation. The redemption of the Acadian people will, in fact, also redeem Great Britain and enhance its reputation as a champion of human rights in the world community. Shortly after the Royal Proclamation was issued, Canadian Senator and Acadian descendant Gerald Comeau called upon the Canadian government to open a new inquiry to determine exactly who ordered the Acadian deportation in order to posthumously sanction those persons. On August 11, 2004, the author met with Senator Comeau at his home in Church Point, Nova Scotia, where he stated his intention to officially request a government investigation of the deportation.

It remains to be seen, in a post-9/11 world, what course the United States will follow in order to be able to maintain the moral authority it has always possessed to stand in judgment of others. In May, 2004, with the discovery of the abuses of prisoners by United States' armed forces in Afghanistan and at the Abu Ghraib prison in Iraq, as well as the disclosure of government memos that appeared to justify torture as an interrogation technique, the United States' reputation in protecting human rights has been considerably damaged. When considering the United States' actions in 2004 and Great Britain's actions in the eighteenth century, we find parallel political agendas which seem to have placed more importance upon those political agendas rather than on protecting human rights. The Royal Proclamation now stands as a model for all countries in the twenty-first century.

Since the signing of the Royal Proclamation, Germany became the next country to acknowledge historical wrongs: on August 1, 2004, in a gesture of humility, German Chancellor Gehard Schroeder bowed on the steps of a memorial to the Warsaw Uprising against Nazi occupation, acknowledging the "immeasurable suffering" inflicted by Germans when they crushed the revolt sixty years ago. Schroeder became the first German chancellor to attend an anniversary of the two-month long uprising, which ended with two hundred thousand Warsaw residents dead and most of the city systematically destroyed by the Nazis. Remembrance of the sixty-three day battle against Nazi troops by Poland's poorly armed and out-manned Home Army resistance movement provoked an outpouring of patriotism in Poland, by civilians and even children.

By repudiating the wrongs committed during the exile, the Crown has sent a clear message that such actions are wrong. Arguably, in a time of peace, there has never been a tragedy with more unnecessary human suffering than the Acadian exile. In his poem *Evangeline*, Longfellow wrote that it was an "exile without end." [109] With the signing of the Royal Proclamation, an end has been symbolically declared. *Beausoleil* and the Acadian people have been redeemed.

EPILOGUE

The Cajun people have evolved dramatically since Joseph Broussard *dit Beausoleil*'s lifetime. Would he recognize today's Cajuns as his descendants? We can only speculate. Certainly, however, the Cajuns of the early twentieth century differed relatively little from their Acadian ancestors. Like the exiles, Cajuns before the mid-twentieth century primarily spoke French and worked as subsistence farmers; if not farmers, they held other folk occupations, such as trapping, fishing, moss-picking, logging, and boat-building.

Around 1940, however, the Cajuns' world began to change with increasing rapidity: the engine of change was World War II. Unlike previous historical events, this global conflict and its aftermath served as major Americanizing agents in south Louisiana, resulting, for instance, in the near demise of Cajun French by the end of the century: in 1990 only about 30 percent of Cajuns spoke the dialect as their first language, and most of these were middle-aged or elderly. Practically no Cajun youths spoke the dialect, even as a second language.

The unifying thread of recent Cajun history *is* Americanization—the process of becoming like the Anglo-American establishment that has traditionally dominated the nation's mainstream culture. Americanization meant embracing the work ethic, materialism, and patriotism of Anglo-America, all of which were foreign to the majority of Cajuns before World War II. It also meant *speaking English*, despite the fact that the Cajuns and their forebears had spoken French as their primary (and usually only) language since coming to America three centuries earlier.

Americanization thus ranks as one of the most important events in the entire Cajun experience, along with the expulsion of their ancestors from Nova Scotia, and south Louisiana's devastation during the Civil War. These events resulted in fundamental changes that forever altered the nature of the ethnic group.

Beginning in the 1960's, however, the Cajuns, swept up in the national trend of ethnic pride and empowerment, mobilized to save their culture. The rise of a grassroots Cajun pride movement and a parallel, more organized movement led by CODOFIL (the Council for Development of French in Louisiana) signaled the Cajuns' efforts to reclaim their heritage through a variety of measures: from protecting the French language in the state constitution of 1974, to demanding in the 1990's that the British government atone for its treatment of the Cajuns' ancestors.

It was in regard to the latter measure that Warren Perrin first made his mark as a Cajun activist. Born in rural Vermilion Parish, Louisiana, to a working-class family, Perrin became seriously interested in his heritage during the late 1980's, when a national event converted him into a militant cultural activist. That event was the passage of the Civil Liberties Act of 1988, which apologized for America's internment of about 120,000 U.S. citizens and resident aliens of Japanese ancestry during World War II.

Perrin found that the Acadian expulsion had not only been illegal according to international law of the period, but that the expulsion order had never been repealed—meaning that Cajun tourists in Canada were technically defying a centuries-old military edict and were subject to prosecution. "We can't close that chapter of our history with this hanging over us," Perrin explained in 1995, "or we will live in exile forever." Declaring the expulsion an overt case of "ethnic cleansing," Perrin used his legal skills to rectify a historical wrong: On behalf of the millions of living Acadian descendants in south Louisiana, Canada, and elsewhere, he prepared a class-action lawsuit titled *Warren A. Perrin et al. v. Great Britain et al.* Known by supporters simply as "the Petition," the suit called on the British government to acknowledge the expulsion.

Perrin's campaign quickly elevated him to the pantheon of leading Cajun activists, a position he further secured when he founded the Acadian Museum in Erath and its support organization, the Acadian Heritage and Culture Foundation. In 1994, he accepted Governor Edwards' invitation to serve as head of CODOFIL, a position that permitted him not only to advance his Petition, but to steer the organization in a new direction.

While making CODOFIL more democratic and more accessible to the general public, Perrin continued some of the organization's established policies, such as promoting French Immersion and using the organization as a vocal anti-defamation league. Under CODOFIL's aegis, for example, he relentlessly discouraged the use of the word "coonass," considered by many to be the supreme ethnic slur against the Cajun people.

One can see why Warren Perrin would be drawn toward the

character of *Beausoleil* Broussard. Both share similar qualities, such as a desire to lead struggles against perceived injustices — in the case of Broussard, on the frontier as a freedom fighter in defense of pioneer Acadian families; in the case of Perrin, in the courtroom as an attorney for average, ordinary plaintiffs, and in the civic arena as a cultural activist for the Cajun people, fighting to save their culture from the steamroller of Americanization.

Beausoleil Broussard undoubtedly would look on with approval as Perrin declares, as he so often does, *"La bataille continue et ensemble on est capable"* — The battle continues and together we will prevail.

Shane K. Bernard

Shane K. Bernard holds a Ph.D. in History from Texas A&M University and degrees in English and History from the University of Louisiana at Lafayette. He is author of *The Cajuns: Americanization of a People* and *Swamp Pop: Cajun and Creole Rhythm and Blues.* Dr. Bernard is also a descendant of Alexandre Broussard *dit Beausoleil.*

LES DRAPEAUX RACCONTENT L'HISTOIRE ACADIENNE DE LA LOUISIANE

FLAGS TELL THE HISTORY OF LOUISIANA'S ACADIANS

Résidence des Acadiens Acadians' location	Pays/États Country/State	Drapeaux Flag
Acadie Acadia (1604 - 1710)	France	"Français à fleur de lys" "Lillies of the Bourdons"
Nouvelle-Écosse Nova Scotia (1710-1763)	Angleterre England	"Union Jack du Roi George II" "King George II's Union Jack"
Colonies Britaniques British Colonies (1755-1763)	Angleterre England	"Union Jack du Roi George II" "King George II's Union Jack"
France (1763-1785)	France	"Français à fleur de lys"
Louisiane Louisiana	Espagne Spain	"L'espagnol des Bourbons" "Bourbon King"
Louisiane Louisiana (novembre 30 - déecembre 20, 1803)	France	"Tricolor français" "Tricolor of the Republic"
Louisiane Louisiana (1803 - 1961)	États Unis United States	"La bannière étoilée" "Stars and Stripes"
République de Louisiane Republic of Louisiana (janvier 1861)	Amérique America	"Le Pélican" "The Pelican"
Républicque de Louisiane Republic of Louisiana (févier 1861)	Amérique America	"Louisiane Indépendante" "The Independence Flag"
Les États Confédérés du sud Confederate States	Amérique America	"La bannière étoilée" "Stars and Bars"

LES DRAPEAUX RACCONTENT L'HISTOIRE ACADIENNE DE LA LOUISIANE

FLAGS TELL THE HISTORY OF LOUISIANA'S ACADIANS

Résidence des Acadiens / Acadians' location	Pays/États / Country/State	Drapeaux / Flag
États Unis United States (1865 - Présent)	États Unis United States	"La gloire de nos ancêtres" "Old Glory"
Louisiane Louisiana	Louisiane Louisiana	"Le Pélican" "The Pelican"
Louisiane Louisiana	Louisiane Louisiana	"La Louisiane Acadienne" "Louisiana Acadian"
Louisiane Louisiana	International International	"Le National Acadien" "National Acadian"

Edité par: René Babineaux et Wilfred Doucette
Dorits d'auteur reservés à La Fondation Culturell du Patrimoine Acadien le 19 mars 1996
Copyright on March 19, 1996 by the Acadian Heritage & Culture Foundation, Inc.

Acadian History In Brief

by: Warren A. Perrin
A Five-Hundred Year Chronology (each year ending with the number 4)

INTRODUCTION: 1504-1604

1504 - The first recorded confirmation of a French fishing vessel on the Grand Banks off Newfoundland;

1524 - A peasants' revolt in the German province of Swabia produces twelve demands, ten of them secular, that graphically illustrate the political problems of the day. They demand abolition of serfdom and the system of "tithe" payments from their crops; removal of restrictions on hunting or fishing on nobles' land reserves; regulation of overlords' often excessive punishments; and the training of priests responsive to their own unique personal and community needs. These demands seek restoration of the social order that prevailed before Catholic feudalism, and suggest the motivation for early Acadian immigration: escape from Christian religious and political oppression;

1534 - A momentous year: Paul III becomes Pope and attempts to rebuild the Church to counteract the Reformation. Jacques Cartier sets out for the New World, attempting, to find a quick route to China. He discovers Prince Edward Island and the coast of New Brunswick, where he makes contact with the Micmac Indians.

Four Hundred Years (1604-2004)

1604 - Samuel Champlain establishes a colony with 79 men at St. Croix on the Bay of Fundy, Nova Scotia, the beginning of *Acadie*;

1654 - The first rudimentary counsel of colonists is established, headed by Guillaume Trahan;

1684 - The first Church is established at Grand Pré; in 1699, Champlain establishes the colony of Louisiana;

1704 - The French and English accelerate military action against each other;

1714 - Queen Anne's Edict allows the Acadians the choice of remaining in the colony or leaving with their possessions. Those who remain become British subjects; the first permanent European settlement in Louisiana is established at Natchitoches;

1724 - The first *Code Noir* is adopted in Louisiana, requiring, among other things, that all slaves be baptized Catholics;

1734 - The infamous Abbé Jean-Louis "*Le Loutre*" (The Otter) arrives in Fort Beauséjour determined to keep Acadian settlers loyal to the French king. His aggressive activities are conceded by most historians to have been the principal cause of much of New England's paranoia about the loyalties of the Acadians to the British;

1754 - April 6-The first fully-documented arrival of Acadian refugees in Louisiana: four families, totaling twenty people, who came via New York. October 29-The Lords of Trade in London caution Lt. Gov. Lawrence of Nova Scotia not to do anything rash with the Acadians. In 1755, Lawrence and the Nova Scotian Council issues expulsion orders which are carried out in September;

1764 - Lord Halifax refuses to permit return of Acadian refugees to Quebec or Acadia thus, the order of deportation is continued in effect. New Brunswick is separated from Nova Scotia;

1794 - First newspaper published in Louisiana, *Le Moniteur de la Louisiane,* in New Orleans;

1814 - Andrew Jackson prepares for the Battle of New Orleans against the British with a ragtag militia reinforced with large numbers of Cajun volunteers. In 1815 the British are defeated;

1824 - The *Marquis de Lafayette* plans a hero's visit to New Orleans. In 1825, Louisiana adopts the *Code Napoléon* for its legal system.

Ten-Year Intervals

1864 - Confederate forces win the Civil War Battle of Mansfield, but lose Acadian General Alfred Mouton;

1874 - Plans are made for the establishment first public schools for Cajuns;

1884 - In follow-up to a Acadian convention in Miscouche, Acadians adopt the official Acadian flag;

1894 - Influx of immigrants to America leads to an anti-immigrant policy resulting in an unsuccessful movement to make English the official language of U. S.; In 1890, the *Université Sainte-Anne* is established by Acadians as the only bi-lingual college in Nova Scotia;

1904 - In 1901, oil is discovered in Louisiana near Jennings; workers from neighboring states move to Louisiana to work in the "oil patch";

1914 - World War I is the beginning of the Americanization of Cajuns;

1924 - Compulsory education is adopted and French-speaking on public school grounds in Louisiana is prohibited; the Longfellow Park movement began, resulting in the creation of the state's first park, "Evangeline Longfellow State Commemorative Area" in St. Martinville in 1930;

1934 - Published government reports identify the Cajuns as the nation's "last unassimilated minority"; on January 19, 1938, Pope Pius XI designates August 15th (Feast Day of the Assumption), as the National Day of the Acadians (*Fête Nationale de l'Acadie*);

1944 - The beginning of the end of World War II and return to Louisiana of servicemen accelerates the Americanization of Cajuns;

1954 - A Louisiana Commission is formed under the direction of Dean Thomas Arceneaux to organize the Acadian Bicentennial Celebration in 1955, commemorating the 200th anniversary of the Acadian deportation;

1964 - *Life Magazine* article: "Waning Echoes From Cajun Country" predicts the demise of the French culture ("there will be no French found in Louisiana by 2000") which inspires the creation of CODOFIL in 1968;

1974 - CODOFIL sponsors the first tribute to Cajun music; the event evolves into *Festivals Acadien*;

1984 - The World's Fair was celebrated in New Orleans which helped to introduce Cajun culture to the rest of the world. Thus, making "Cajun" trendy. In 1990, a Petition was delivered to the British Government and Queen Elizabeth requesting an apology for the Acadian deportation;

1994 - First *Congrès Mondial Acadien* is held in New Brunswick, Canada; the second *Congrès Mondial Acadien Louisiane* is held in 1999 in conjunction with *FrancoFête '99*, the tricentennial celebration of the founding of the French colony of Louisiana. On December 9, 2003, a Royal Proclamation was signed acknowledging the wrongs with occurred during the Acadian deportation;

2004 - The third *Congrès Mondial Acadien 2004* is held in Nova Scotia commemorating the 400th anniversary of the founding of Acadia. Under the leadership of Shelia Broussard, the Broussard Family Reunion is held in Pomquet, Nova Scotia from August 11-13th, organized by the Famille Broussard Family Society.

PETITION OF THE ACADIANS DEPORTED TO PHILADELPHIA TO THE KING OF ENGLAND

As this is the Acadians' defense in this tragedy, written by them, we print the entire petition translated from French.

"To His Most Excellent Majesty, King of Great Britain, etc., etc.

"The humble petition of his subjects, the last French inhabitants of Nova Scotia, formerly settled on the Bay of Minas, the rivers thereunto belongings; now residing in the Province of Pennsylvania, on behalf of themselves and the rest of the last inhabitants of the said bay, and also of those formerly settled on the river of Annapolis Royal, wheresoever dispersed.

"May it please Your Majesty.

"It is not in our power sufficiently to trace back the conditions upon which our ancestors first settled in Nova Scotia, under the protection of Your Majesty's predecessors, as the great part of our elders who were acquainted with these transactions are dead; but more specially because our papers, which contained our contracts, records, etc., etc., were, by violence, taken from us some time before the unhappy catastrophe which has been the occasion of the calamities we are now under; but we always understood the foundation thereof to be from an agreement made between Your Majesty's Commanders in Nova Scotia and our forefathers about the year 1713, whereby they were permitted to remain in the possession of their lands, under an oath of fidelity to the British Government, with an exemption from bearing arms, and the allowance of the free exercise of our religion.

"It is a matter of certainty,—and within the compass of some of our memories—that in the year 1730, General Philipps, the Governor of Nova Scotia, did, in your Majesty's name, confirm unto us, and all the inhabitants of the whole extent of the Bay of Minas and rivers thereunto belonging, the free and entire possession of those lands we were then possessed of; which, by grants from the former French Government, we held to us and our heirs forever, on paying the customary quit-rents, etc., and on condition that we should behave with due submission and fidelity to Your Majesty, agreeable to the oath which was then administered to us, which is as follows, viz: 'We sincerely promise and swear, by the faith of a Christian, that we shall be entirely faithful, and will truly submit ourselves to His Majesty King George, whom we acknowledge as sovereign Lord of New Scotland, or Acadia; so help us.'

"And at the same time, the said General Philipps did, in like manner, promise the said French inhabitants, in Your Majesty's name that they should have the true exercise of their religion, and be exempted from bearing arms, and from being employed in war, either against the French or Indians. Under the sanction of this solemn engagement we held our lands, made further purchases, annually paying our quit-rents, etc., and we had the greatest reason to conclude that Your Majesty did not disapprove of the above agreement, and that our conduct continued, during a long course of years, to be such as recommended us to your gracious protection, and to the regard of the Governor of New England, appears from a printed declaration, made seventeen years after this time, by His Excellency William S. Shirley, Governor of New England, which was published and dispersed in our country, some copies of which have escaped from the general destruction of most of our papers, part of which follows:

" 'By His Majesty's command,

" 'A declaration of William Shirley, Esq., Captain-General and Governor-in-Chief, in and over His Majesty's Province of Massachusetts' Bay, etc.

" 'To His Majesty's subjects, the French inhabitants of his province of Nova Scotia: Whereas, upon being informed that a report had been propagated among His Majesty's subjects, the French inhabitants of his Province of Nova Scotia, that there was an intention to remove them from their settlements in that Province, I did, by my declaration dated 16th September, 1746, signify to them that the same was groundless, and that I was, on the contrary, persuaded that His Majesty would be graciously pleased to extend his royal protection to all such of them as should continue in their fidelity and allegiance to him, and in no wise abet or hold correspondence with the enemies of his Crown; and therein assured them, that I would make a favorable representation of their state and circumstances to His Majesty, and did accordingly transmit a representation thereof to be laid before him, and have thereupon received his royal pleasure, touching his aforesaid subjects in Nova Scotia, with his express command to signify the same to them in his name: now, by virtue thereof, and in obedience to His Majesty's said orders, I do hereby declare, in His Majesty's name, that there is not the least foundation for any apprehensions of His Majesty's intending to remove them, the said inhabitants of Nova Scotia, from their said settlements and habitations within the said Province; but that, on the contrary, it is His Majesty's resolution to protect and maintain all such of them as have adhered to and shall continue in their duty and allegiance to him, in the quiet and peaceable possession of their respective habitations and settlements, and in the enjoyment of their rights and privileges as his subjects, etc., etc.

"'Dated at Boston, the 21st of October, 1747.' "And this is further confirmed by a letter, dated 29th, of June, in the same year, written to our deputies by Mr. Mascarene, then Your Majesty's chief commander in Nova Scotia, which refers to Governor Shirley's first declaration, of which we have a copy, legally authenticated, part of which is as follows, viz:

"'As to the fear you say you labor under, on account of being threatened to evacuate the country, you have in possession His Excellency William Shirley's printed l e t t e r, of September 16, 1746 whereby you may be made easy in that respect: you are sensible of the promises I have made to you, the effects of which you have already felt, that I would protect you so long as, by your conduct and fidelity to the Crown of Great Britain, you would enable me to do so, which promise I do again repeat to you.'

"At the time of the publication of the above declaration, it was required that our deputies should, on behalf of all the people, renew the oath formerly taken to General Philipps, which was done without any mention of bearing arms, and we can with truth say, that we are not sensible of alternation in our disposition and conduct since that time, but that we always continued to retain a grateful regard to Your Majesty and your Government, notwithstanding which, we have found ourselves surrounded with difficulties unknown to us before. Your Majesty determined to fortify our Province and settle Halifax; which the French looking upon with jealousy, they made frequent incursions through our country, in order to annoy that settlement, whereby we came exposed to many straits and hardships; yet, from the obligations we were under, from the oath we had taken, we were never under any doubt, but that it was our indispensable duty and interest, to remain true to your Government and our oath of fidelity, hoping that in time those difficulties would be removed and we should see peace and tranquility restored; and if, from the change of affairs in Nova Scotia, Your Majesty had thought it not inconsistent with the safety of your said Province to let us remain there upon the terms promised us by your Governors, in Your Majesty's name, we should doubtless have acquiesced with any other reasonable proposal which might have been made to us, consistent with the safety of our aged parents, and tender wives and children; and we are persuaded, if that had been the case, wherever we had retired, we should have held ourselves under the strongest obligations of gratitude, from a thankful remembrance of the happiness we had enjoyed under Your Majesty's administration and gracious protection. About the time of the settlement of Halifax, General Cornwallis, Governor of Nova Scotia, did require that we should take the oath of allegiance without the exemption before allowed us of not bearing arms; but this we absolutely refused, as being an infringement of the principal condition upon which our forefathers agreed to settle under the British Government.

"And we acquainted Governor Cornwallis, that if Your Majesty was not willing to continue that exemption to us, we desired liberty to evacuate the country, proposing to settle on the Island of St. John, where the French Government was willing to let us have land; which proposal he at that time refused to consent to, but told us he would acquaint Your Majesty therewith and return us an answer. But we never received an answer, nor was any proposal of that made to us until we were made prisoners.

"After the settlement of Halifax we suffered many abuses and insults from Your Majesty's enemies, more specially from the Indians in the interest of the French, by whom our cattle was killed, our houses pillaged, and many of us personally abused and put in fear of our lives, and some even carried away prisoners towards Canada, solely on account of our resolution steadily to maintain our oath of fidelity to the English Government; particularly Rene LeBlanc— our public notary—was taken prisoner by the Indians when actually travelling in Your Majesty's service, his house pillaged, and himself carried to the French fort, from whence he did not recover his liberty but with great difficulty, after four years captivity.

"We were likewise obliged to comply with the demand of the enemy, made for provisions, cattle, etc., etc., upon pain of military execution, which we had reason to believe the Government was made sensible was not an act of choice on our part, but of necessity, as those in authority appeared to take in good part the representations we always made to them after anything of that nature had happened.

"Notwithstanding the many difficulties we thus laboured under, yet we dare appeal to the several Governors, both at Halifax and Annapolis Royal, for testimonies of our being always ready and willing to obey their orders, and give all the assistance in our power, either in furnishing provisions and materials or making roads, building forts, etc., etc., agreeable to Your Majesty's orders, and our oath of fidelity, whensoever called upon, or required thereunto.

"It was also our constant care to give notice to Your Majesty's commanders, of the danger they from time to time have been exposed to by the enemy's troops, and had the intelligence we gave been always attended to, many lives might have been spared, particularly in the unhappy affair which befell Major Noble and his brother at Grand Pre, when they, with great numbers of their men, were cut off by the enemy, notwithstanding the frequent advices we had given them of the danger they were in; and yet we have been very unjustly accused as parties in that massacre.

"And although we have been thus anxiously concerned to manifest our fidelity in these several respects, yet it has been falsely insinuated, that it had been our general practice to abet and support Your Majesty's enemies; but we trust that your Majesty will not suffer suspicions and accusations to be received as proof sufficient to reduce thousands of innocent people, from the most happy situation to a state of the greatest distress and misery. No, this was far from our thoughts; we esteemed our situation so happy as by no means to desire a change.

"We have always desired, and again desire that we may be permitted to answer our accusers in a judicial way. In the meantime permit us, sir, here solemnly to declare, that these accusations are utterly false and groundless, so far as they concern us as a collective body of people. It hath been always our desire to live as our fathers have done, as faithful subjects under Your Majesty's royal protection, with an unfeigned resolution to maintain our oath of fidelity to the utmost of our power. Yet it cannot be expected but that amongst us, as well as amongst other people, there have been some weak and false-hearted persons, susceptible to being bribed by the enemy so as to break the oath of fidelity. Twelve of these were outlawed in Governor Shirley's Proclamation before mentioned; but it will be found that the number of such falsehearted men amongst us were very few, considering our situation, the number of our inhabitants, and how we stood circumstanced in several respects; and it may easily be made to appear that it was the constant care of our Deputies to prevent and put a stop to such wicked conduct when it came to their knowledge.

"We understand that the aid granted to the French by the inhabitants of Beaubassin has been used as an argument to accelerate our ruin; but we trust that Your Majesty will not permit the innocent to be involved with the guilty; no consequence can be justly drawn, that, because those people yielded to the threats and persuasions of the enemy we should do the same. They were situated so far from Halifax as to be in a great measure out of the protection of the English Government, which was not our case; we were separated from them by sixty miles of uncultivated land, and no other connection with them than what is usual with neighbors at such a distance; and we can truly say, we looked on their defection from Your Majesty's interest with great pain and anxiety. Nevertheless, not long before our being made prisoners, the house in which we kept our contracts, records, deeds, etc., was invested with an armed force, and all our papers violently carried away, none of which have to this day been returned to us, whereby we are in a great measure deprived of means of making our innocence and the justness of our complaints appear in their true light.

"Upon our sending a remonstrance to the Governor and Council, of the violence that had been offered us by the seizure of our papers, and the groundless fears the Government appeared to be under on our account, by their taking away our arms, no answer was returned to us; but those who had signed the remonstrance, and some time after sixty more, in all about eighty of our elders were summoned to appear before the Governor in Council, which they immediately complied with; and it was required of them that they should take the oath of allegiance without the exemption which, during a course of nearly fifty years, has been granted to us and to our fathers, of not being obliged to bear arms, and which was the principal condition upon which our ancestors agreed to remain in Nova Scotia, when the rest of the inhabitants evacuated the country; which, as it was contrary to our inclination and judgment, we thought ourselves engaged in duty absolutely to refuse. Nevertheless, we freely offered, and would gladly have renewed our oath of fidelity, but this was not accepted, and we were all immediately made prisoners, and were told by the Governor, that our estates, both real and personal, were forfeited for Your Majesty's use. As to those who remained at home, they were summoned to appear before the commanders in the forts, which, we showing some fear to comply with, on account of the seizure of our papers, and imprisonment of so many of our elders, we had the greatest assurance given us, that there was no other design but to make us renew our former oath of fidelity; yet, as soon as we were within the fort, the same judgement was passed on us as had been passed on our brethen at Halifax, and we were also made prisoners.

"Thus, notwithstanding the solemn grants made to our fathers by General Philipps, and the declaration made by Governor Shirley and M. Mascarene in Your Majesty's name, that it was Your Majesty's resolution to protect and maintain all such of us as should continue in their duty and allegiance to Your Majesty, in the quiet and peaceable possession of their settlements, and the enjoyment of all their rights and privileges as Your Majesty's subjects; we found ourselves at once deprived of our liberties, without any judicial process or even without any accusers appearing against us, and this solely grounded on mistaken jealousies and false suspicions that we are inclinable to take part with Your Majesty's enemies. But we again declare that that accusation is groundless; it was our fixed resolution to maintain, to the utmost of our power, the oath of fidelity which we had taken, not only from a sense of indispensable duty but also because we were well satisfied with our situation under Your Majesty's Government and protection, and did not think it could be bettered by any change which could be proposed to us. It has also been falsely insinuated that we held the opinion that we might be absolved from our oath so as to break it with impunity, but this we likewise solemnly declare to be a false accusation, and which we plainly evinced by our exposing ourselves to so great losses and sufferings rather than take the oath proposed by the Governor and Council, because we apprehended we could not in conscience comply therewith.

"Thus we, our ancient parents and grandparents—men of great integrity and approved fidelity to Your Majesty—and our innocent wives and children, became the unhappy victims to those groundless fears; we were transported into the English colonies, and this was done in such haste, and with so little regard to our necessities and the tenderest ties of nature, that from the most social enjoyments, and affluent circumstances, many found themselves destitute of the necessities of life. Parents were separated from children, husbands from wives, some of whom have not to this day met again; and we were so crowded in the transport vessels, that we had not room even for all our bodies to lay down at once, and consequently were prevented from carrying with us proper necessities, especially for the support and comfort of the aged and weak, many of whom quickly ended their misery with their lives. And even those amongst us who had suffered deeply from Your Majesty's enemies, on account of their attachment to Your Majesty's Government, were equally involved in the common calamity of which Rene LeBlanc, the Notary Public before mentioned, is a remarkable instance. He was seized, confined, and brought away among the rest of the people, and his family, consisting of twenty children, and about one hundred and fifty grandchildren, were scattered in different colonies, so that he was put on shore at New York, with only his wife and two youngest children, in an infirm state of health, from whence he joined three more of his children, at Philadelphia, where he died without any more notice being taken of him than any of us, notwithstanding his many years' labor and deep sufferings for Your Majesty's service.

"The miseries we have since endured are scarce sufficiently to be expressed, being reduced for a livelihood to toil at hard labor in a southern clime, so disagreeable to our constitutions that most of us have been prevented by sickness from procuring the necessary subsistence for our families; and therefore are threatened with that which we esteem the greatest aggravation of all our sufferings, even of having our children forced from us, and bound out to strangers and exposed to contagious distempers unknown in our native country.

"This, compared with the affluence and ease we enjoyed, shows our condition to be extremely wretched. We have already seen in this Province of Pennsylvania two hundred and fifty of our people, which is more than half the number that were landed here, perish through misery and various diseases. In this great distress and misery, we have, under God, none but Your Majesty to look to with hopes of relief and redress:

"We therefore hereby implore your gracious protection, and request you may be pleased to let the justice of our complaints be truly and impartially inquired into, and that Your Majesty would please to grant us such relief, as in your justice and clemency you will think our case requires, and we shall hold ourselves bound to pray, etc."

NOTES

CHAPTER 1 - THE FIRST BROUSSARD IN ACADIA

1. The Associated Press, "Maine Celebrating French Connection," *CNN.com*, June 23, 2004. On June 26, 2004, dignitaries from France, Canada and the United States marked the 400th anniversary on St. Croix Island, Maine. An estimated 18 million people of French descent now live on the North American continent, including some who trace their roots to Acadians expelled by the British in 1755. Yet while they are participating in the event, the Passamaquoddy Indians view white man's arrival as a watershed event that brought tragedy to the Indians.

2. Geoffrey Plank, *An Unsettled Conquest* (University of Pennsylvania Press, Philadelphia, Pennsylvania, 2001), p. 19.

3. Clément Cormier, "Jean-François Brossard (Broussard)," in *Dictionnaire Biographique du Canada* Vol. III (10 vols.; Quebec, 1974), where he is described as a "ploughman and settler." Although it is written that his name was "Jean-François" and he sailed on the ship *l'Orange* from La Rochelle, France in 1671 along with 50 other French colonists, Stephen White, eminent Acadian geneologist, has found this not to be correct, i.e., his given name was "François", not "Jean-François," as recorded in several instances, and he did not sail to *Acadie* on *l'Orange*, but was probably born in *Acadie*. He was not listed in the census of 1671 of *Acadie*, but it is known that the census that year was not complete. White believes that Alexandre was the "brains" and *Beausoleil* the "brawn". The parents of Francois Broussard are unknown. Stephen White, lecture to the Broussard Family Reunion, Pomquet, Nova Scotia, August 13, 2004.

4. Vita B. Reaux and John R. Reaux, "Jean François Broussard and Catherine Richard," *Attakapas Gazette*, 6 (March, 1971), pp. 4-18.

5. Genealogy provided by Mitch Conover, member of *La Famille Beausoleil* and noted Acadian genealogist from Lafayette, Louisiana. The historiography supporting the Broussard Coat of Arms states:

"The surname Broussard appears to be characteristic, in origin, and is believed to be associated with the French, meaning 'one having disheveled hair'."

6. Andrew Hill Clark, *Acadia: The Geography of Early Nova Scotia to 1760* (University of Wisconsin Press, 1968).

7. Daniel N. Paul, *We Were Not Savages: A Micmac Perspective on the Collision of European and Aboriginal Civilization* (Nimbus Publishing, Ltd., 1993) and Daniel N. Paul, "Mi'Kmaq, Acadians: friends then and now," *The Halifax Herald*, June 9, 2004, p. 1. Note that the spelling of the word used in the text to refer to the aboriginal people is "Mi'Kmaq" and not "Micmac."

8. Ibid., footnote 2, Chapter 3, pp. 68-105.

9. Acadian Senator Viola Leger, in an address to Canadian Senate Chamber, *News From the Senate*, Vol. 1, No. 3, June, 2004, and Roland F. Surette, *Métis/Acadian Heritage 1604*-2004 (Sentinel Printing Limited, Yarmouth, Nova Scotia, 2004). Surette contends that *Beausoleil*'s maternal great-great-grandmother was a Mi'Kmaq.

10. Emery J. Broussard and Lorraine Broussard Campbell, in *Vermilion Historical Society, History of Vermilion Parish, Louisiana, Vol. II*, "Jean-François Broussard" and "Joseph *dit Beausoleil* Broussard," *Vermilion Historical Society* (Dallas: Taylor Publishing Co., 2003), 2:43-44.

CHAPTER 2 - THE EARLY YEARS: COLONIZATION

11. Dudley J. LeBlanc, *The True Story of the Acadians* (By author, Lafayette, Louisiana, 1937).

12. C.J. d'Entremont, "Joseph Brossard (Broussard) *dit Beausoleil*," in *Dictionnaire Biographique du Canada*, Vol. III , De 1741 à 1770 (Toronto, Canada, 1974), p. 93, and Glenn Conrad, edited, *A Dictionary of Louisiana Biography*, "Joseph dit *Beausoleil* Broussard" (Louisiana Historical Association and Center for Louisiana Studies, University of Southwestern Louisiana, Lafayette, Louisiana, 1988), Vol. I, p. 115.

13. J.C. Webster, *The Life of Thomas Pichon.*

14. Daniel N. Paul, *The Confrontation of Micmac and European Civilizations* (Truro, 1993).

15. Ibid., footnote 6, p. 77.

CHAPTER 3 - *BEAUSOLEIL'S* FOUR CIVIL DISPUTES

16. John B. Brebner, *New England Outpost: Acadia Before the Conquest of Canada* (Columbia University Press, New York, 1927), p. 41.

17. Maurice Basque, *"Conflits Et Solidarités Familiales Dams : Ancienne Acadie: L'Affaire Broussard De 1724,"* La Société Historique Acadienne, Les Cahiers, Vol. 20, No. 2, *Avril-Juin* 1989, pp. 60-68. Translated by Jean Ouellet.

18. Paul Surette, *"La prée de l'Île et le Village-des-Beausoleil,"* in *Atlas de L'Etablissement des Acadiens aux Trois Rivieres du Chignectou, 1660-1785* (Editions d'Acadie, Moncton, 1996), p. 234. Translated by Jean Ouellet and Dr. Jean-Douglas Comeau.

19. Maurice Basque, *"Genre et gestion du pouvoir communautaire á Annapolis Royal au 18e siècle,"* Dalhousie Law Journal, Vol. 17, No. 2, Fall 1994, pp. 498-508. Translation by Jean Ouellet.

20. Original minutes of His Majesty's Council at Annapolis Royale, 1720 - 1739, edited by A. M. Mack Mehan, Halifax, *Public Archives of Nova Scotia,* 1908, p.113.

21. Ibid, p. 113.

CHAPTER 4 - THE RESISTANCE

22. Ronnie-Gilles LeBlanc, *Joseph Broussard* dit *Beausoleil (Cahiers de la Societé historique Acadienne* 52, 1986), Vol. 17, No. 2, p. 52.

23. Jean Ségalen, *Acadie en résistance* (Skal Vreigh-Montroules/Morlaix, France, 2002).

24. Jim Bradshaw, "UL Lafayette Acquires 1755 Letter," *The Daily Advertiser,* October 20, 2001. On October 2, 2001, due to the cooperation of Zachary Richard (who learned that the letter was available for purchase) and Dr. Carl A. Brasseaux, the University of Louisiana at Lafayette announced acquisition of the historically significant Winslow letter.

25. John Winslow, "Winslow's Journals," *Collections of the Nova Scotia Historical Society,* Boston, Massachusetts.

26. Henri-Dominique Paratte, *Peoples of the Maritimes - Acadians* (Nimbus Publishing, Toronto, California, 1998), p. 42.

27. Gladys Trenholm, Miep Norden and Josephine Trenholm, *A History of Fort Lawrence* (Sherwood Printing Ltd., Edmonton, Alberta, Canada, 1985), p. 78.

28. Ibid., footnote 6, p. 105.

29. Ibid., footnote 27, p. 87.

30. Peter L. McCreath and John G. Leefe, *History of Early Nova Scotia* (Four East Publishing, Tentallon, Nova Scotia, 1982).

31. Ibid.   On August 8, 1755, Lawrence sent a letter to Colonel Monckton which seemed to indicate that he was far more interested in the cattle of the Acadians than in preserving the lives of the unsuspecting inhabitants, "...I would have all care taken to save the stock and the harvest..." Canadian Archives, vol. II, Appendix B, p. 8 (1905).

32. James Hannay, *The History of Acadia* (J.&A. McMillan, St. John, New Brunswick, 1879), p. 411.

33. Jim Bradshaw, "Broussard Led Acadians to Attakapas Area," *The Daily*

Advertiser, Supplement: History of Acadiana, March 20, 1999, p. 18.

34. Paul Surette, *"Petcoudiac"* (*Les Editions d'Acadie,* Moncton, New Brunswick, 1988). "On the question whether Joseph *Beausoleil* Broussard escaped from Fort Lawrence: We know he was arrested -- at least Thomas Pichon (French official at Beausejour spying for the British) said so. [Pichon to Bulkeley or Henshelwood, 9/26/1755: 'I prevented the Brossards [Broussard], called *Beausoleil,* whose families are numerous, as well as other inhabitants of Petkoudiac from the side of Rivièère Saint-Jean, from abandoning their possessions to go join the Malecites and Abenakis, who considered them their bravest brothers. These *Beausoleils* have since been arrested.' *Collection de documents inédits* 2:127-131] We know that as early as the fall of 1755 Joseph *Beausoleil* Broussard was a leader of the Acadian resistance. Certainly, the British didn't voluntarily release him from custody. We also know that a group of Acadians escaped from Fort Lawrence on the night of October 1, 1755. Joseph *Beausoleil* Broussard is not mentioned in the contemporary evidence as being among them, but that evidence doesn't give the names of any of the escapees. That's the best I can do. We know Joseph *Beausoleil* Broussard was arrested and incarcerated along with his brother Alexandre, and probably all their adult male children. We know that Alexandre and some other Broussards were exiled to Charles Town, S. C., from where he and one of Joseph's [*Beausoleil's*] sons escaped and made their way back to Acadia. We know that there he joined Joseph [*Beausoleil*] as a leader of the resistance. Thus, I assume it must be the case that Joseph had escaped from British custody, probably on October 1, 1755, which is the only such escape mentioned in the contemporary evidence." Dr. John Mack Faragher, private email to author, September 7, 2004.

35. John Mack Faragher, *A Great and Noble Scheme: The Expulsion of the French Acadians,* a forthcoming book (New York: W.W. Norton, 2005). According to Nova Scotian historical writer Alfred Silver, the weather in Nova Scotia is very unpredictable. "Only those who are very in-tune with the country can read the signs of approaching adverse weather a few days in advance. Therefore, when *Beausoleil* and his fellow prisoners dug their narrow little escape tunnel they

probably knew that there were rainstorms coming that would turn the tunnel walls into mud. This detail explains how the smallest-to-largest gambit worked. It also neatly illustrates one of the few advantages the Acadians had over the British military machine: they knew the country and the climate." Alfred Silver, private letter to author, August 21, 2004.

36. Alton E. Broussard, "Were Early Acadian Men Really The Docile Type?," *The Daily Advertiser*, November, 1977.

37. Angela Simmoneaux, *"All in the Family," The Sunday Advocate*, Baton Rouge, Louisiana, February 28, 1999. According to Dr. John Mack Faragher, the Yankee Benjamin Church employed such method of fighting in the late seventeenth century, and other New Englanders employed these tactics in various engagements with Abenakis.

38. Ibid., footnote 27, p. 90. Emphasis added by author.

39. Carl A. Brasseaux, *Quest for the Promised Land* (University of Southwestern Louisiana Center for Louisiana Studies, 1989), p. 4 at footnote no. 10.

40. R. Brun, "Amherst Papers," *la Societé Historique Acadienne* (Moncton, New Brunswick, 1970), p. 304.

41. Ibid., footnote 27, p. 93

42. Ibid, footnote 40, p. 307.

43. Ibid., footnote 27, p. 94.

44. One of the men surrendering at Fort Cumberland was a Joseph Broussard and most historians have assumed that this was *Beausoleil*. See Arsenault, *History of Acadians,* p. 160. However, according to Maureen G. Arceneaux, in *Acadian to Cajun: Population, Family and Wealth in Southwest Louisiana, 1765-1854,* a dissertation presented to the department of history at Brigham Young University, April, 1982, (*The Historical New Orleans Collection,* New Orleans, La.) at footnote

12, the Amherst Papers clearly refer to *Beausoleil* as being active through December, 1761. Citing: Brum, *Amherst Papers,* p. 307. Alexandre had a son, Joseph, who was an adult at this time, and he may have been the one who accompanied his father into the British fort because the son's widow was at Halifax in 1763 with Alexandre. Also, in July, 1761, *Beausoleil* was identified on a census as living on the Miramichi River. *Amherst Papers,* p. 300.

45. Ibid., footnote 27, p. 94.

46. Janet Jen, *Acadiana Genealogy Exchange,* 863 Wayman Branch Road, Covington, Kentucky, Newsletter, Vol. XXVI, April/July, 1997, p. 49.

CHAPTER 5 - FINALIZING THE ACADIAN PROBLEM

47. Dianne Marshall, *Georges Island - The Keep of Halifax Harbour* (Nimbus Publishing, Halifax, Nova Scotia, 2003), pp. 91-109, and Jeannot Doiron, *Le pays de "la Cadie"* (By author, Canada, 2004).

48. Ibid.

49. Ibid., footnote 26, p. 47.

CHAPTER 6 - DEPARTING FOR A NEW LIFE

50. Alphonse Deveau, *Two Beginnings: A Brief Acadian History* (Lescarbot Publications, Canada,1980), p. 111. "Some Acadians remained in Nova Scotia or later returned to settle in remote areas. The region, known officially as the Municipality of Clare, has the largest concentration of Acadians of any place in Nova Scotia — almost 10,000 residents, about a fourth of the province's Acadian population. Clare was host to the Congrès' opening ceremonies July 31, on the campus of the *Université Sainte-Anne,* Nova Scotia's only French-language university, and then 12 family reunions, including the Comeau and Leblanc gatherings that attracted thousands of people and smaller gatherings for the Robichaud and Dugas families and others." Ron Thibodeaux, "Acadian Homecoming," *The Times-Picayune,* August 22, 2004, p. A20.

51. Carl A. Brasseaux, *The Founding of New Acadia* (Louisiana State University Press, Baton Rouge, 1987), p. 34.

52. Ibid., footnote 39, p. 54.

53. Ibid., footnote 51, p. 74.

54. Carl A. Brasseaux, *Scattered to the Wind: Dispersal and Wanderings of the Acadians, 1755-1809* (University of Southwestern Louisiana, Center for Louisiana Studies, Lafayette, Louisiana, 1991), p. 2.

55. Naomi E.S. Griffiths, *The Acadians: Creation of a People* (McGraw-Hill Ryerson, Ltd., Canada 1973). There are many parallels between *Beausoleil's* life and that of Antoni Chrusciel, the revered leader of a doomed 1944 revolt against Poland's Nazi occupiers. Chrusciel was "Chief" of the Home Army resistance movement in Nazi-occupied Warsaw and commanded the insurgents who rose in revolt against the Germans on August 1, 1944. He lead sixty-three days of fighting, until the resistance gave way to the better-armed enemy. Twenty thousand insurgents died in the uprising and his native town was reduced to rubble. He was captured and held in prison camps in Germany until being liberated by U. S. troops. Like *Beausoleil*, instead of returning to his native land after the war, he choose to live in exile in Britain and moved to the United States in 1956. He died in 1960 at the age of sixty-five. On July 30, 2004, his remains were brought from the United States and finally laid to rest in Warsaw for a ceremonial funeral as part of the 60th anniversary observances of the uprising. *Daily Advertiser*, Associated Press, "Poland brings home hero of 1944 revolt," July 31, 2004.

56. Ibid., footnote 51, p. 34.

CHAPTER 7 - THE SETTLEMENT OF "NEW ACADIA"

57. Grover Rees, translation, "The Dauterive Compact: Foundation of the Cattle Industry," *Attakapas Gazette* 11 (Summer, 1976), p. 91.

58. William Henry Perrin, *Southwest Louisiana Biographical and Historical* (The Gulf Publishing Co., 1891, reprinted by Claitor's Publishing Division, Baton Rouge, La. 1971), p. 189. In this document, *Beausoleil's* first name, Joseph, was improperly listed as "Gaurhept."

59. *St. Martin de Tours* Catholic Church, *Copie d'un vieux registre* Archives, St. Martinville, Louisiana, p. 8. Also see Ibid., footnote 39, p. 34.

60. Ibid., p. 8. Translation by Jean Ouellet. The french word *inhumé* is used and translates as "buried," but may have also meant "cremated."

61. Rev. Donald J. Hebert, *Southwest Louisiana Records,* (Hebert Publications, Louisiana), Volume 1A, p. 137.

62. Carl A. Brasseaux, *Lafayette* (Windsor Publications, Inc., 1990), p. 10. According to George Bentley, Jean Baptiste Broussard, the son of Alexandre Broussard, was buried in St. John's Cathedral Cemetery in Lafayette, Louisiana. Jean Baptiste Broussard had a very full life: he was born in Acadia (circa 1732), participated in and survived the Acadian resistance against the British, migrated to New Orleans with *Beausoleil* where he was a signee of the Dauterive Compact and later acquired an original Spanish land grant in the area of Parks, Louisiana. His headstone reads: "Jean Baptiste Broussard, Rev. War, 1727-1825."

63. Bona Arsenault, History of the Acadians (By Author, Ottawa, Canada, 1988), p. 195. "Soon thereafter, other exiles began trickling into Louisiana, itself a former French colony, where the Spanish government was happy to offer land grants to frontier settlers. About 3,000 Acadians eventually reached Louisiana, adapted to the heat and mosquitos, and laid the groundwork for what would become the state's Cajun culture." Ron Thibodeaux, "Acadian Homecoming," *The Times-Picayune*, August 22, 2004, p. A1.

CHAPTER 8 - THE LEGACY

64. Lucius Fontenot, Lafayette, Louisiana, image protected by Trademark, all rights reserved. Copyright© 2004. To order T-shirts: Acadian Museum, 203 South Broadway, Erath, Louisiana 70533, 337-233-5832, 337-937-5468 or acadianmuseum.com. "Lucius Fontenot had an idea for a T-shirt while one day thinking about the T-shirts with the image of Ernesto 'che' Guevara, the Argentina-born, Cuban revolutionary. Fontenot says, 'I was thinking that the only rebel we have as Cajuns was this guy [*Beausoleil*] Broussard, [and] not a lot of kids know about this bad-ass cat who fought the British.' So Fontenot designed his own T-shirts with the image of Broussard. He says, 'It's to get the younger kids interested in the culture in any way possible.' The back of the T-shirt reads: 'Joseph *Beausoleil* Broussard (1702-1765), Leader of the Acadian Resistance who valiantly fought the British to prevent deportation for Acadians from Nova Scotia. After imprisonment *Beausoleil* led the first Acadians to Louisiana where he became Militia Captain of the Attakapas region." R. Reese Fuller, "Talking About a Revolution," *The Independent,* August 25, 2004, p. 27.

65. J. Alphonse Deveau, *Le Chef des Acadiens* (Les Editions Lescarbrot, Yarmouth, Nova Scotia, 1980), Second Edition, p. 19, where *Beausoleil* is depicted fighting a British Ranger.

66. Antoinine Maillet, *Pélagie,* translated by Phillip Stafford (New Press, 1970), p. 60.

67. Chris Segura, "La Famille Beausoleil Reunion Planned in Concert With Acadian Congress," *The Daily Advertiser,* December 10, 1996.

68. Bliss Carman, *The Vengeance of Noel Broussard - A Tale of the Acadian Expulsion* (The University Press of Cambridge, Massachusetts, 1919), p. 13.

69. Alfred Silver, *Three Hills Home* (Nimbus Publishing Ltd., Halifax, Nova Scotia, 2001), p. 2. Silver and the author made a joint presentation on *Beausoleil* at the Broussard Family Reunion in the

Village of Pomquet, Antigonish County, Nova Scotia, on August 11-13, 2004, in conjunction with the *Congrès Mondial Acadien 2004.* Shelia Broussard, President of the Famille Broussard Family Society, was the principal organizer of the event, which coincided with Canada's celebration of the 400th anniversary of the arrival of the French colonists in North America.

70. James P. Louviere, Ph.D., New Iberia, Louisiana, wrote a song *"Hey, Hey, Beausoleil!"* dedicated to "Joseph Broussard, leader of the resistance to the British invasion of Acadie." Arranged and transcribed by Sarah Roy.

71. Shane K. Bernard, *The Cajuns: Americanization of a People* (University Press of Mississippi, Jackson, Mississippi, 2003), p. 150.

72. Ibid., footnote 12, p. 87.

CHAPTER 9 - THE BROUSSARD CLAN IN LOUISIANA

73. Robert West, *An Atlas of Louisiana Surnames of French and Spanish Origin,* (Geoscience Publications, Louisiana State University, Baton Rouge), pp. 41-43.

74. Harry Lewis Griffin, *A Brief History of the Acadians,* from an address delivered at a meeting of *France-Amerique de la Louisiane Acadienne* at the College of the Sacred Heart, Grand Coteau, Louisiana, October 18, 1952.

75. Paul E. Hoffman, editor, *The Louisiana Purchase and Its People* (Louisiana Historical Association and the Center for Louisiana Studies, University of Louisiana at Lafayette, 2004), p. 117. Regional Editor of *The Daily Advertiser* wrote: "In the early days of settlement, all of what we now call Acadiana was governed locally from two posts — the *Poste des Attakapas* (now St. Martinville) and the *Poste des Opelousas.* William Darby, a geographer who traveled in south Louisiana in 1807, said the boundary between the area governed from Opelousas and the one from the Attakapas post began at the mouth of the Mermentau River and ran to the mouth

of Bayou Queue-de-Tortue. The dividing line followed the bayou to its source, then followed a line from there to the head of Bayou Carencro. It continued down Bayou Carencro to its mouth, then up the Vermilion River to Bayou Fuselier at Arnaudville, then down to Bayou Fuselier's junction with Bayou Teche, then straight east across the Atchafalaya Basin. Everything west of the boundary as far as the Sabine River was in the Opelousas District. This included the present parishes of St. Landry, Evangeline, Acadia, Jefferson Davis, Beauregard, Allen, Calcasieu and part of Cameron. The Attakapas District included what is now St. Martin, St. Mary, Iberia, Lafayette, Vermilion and the part of Cameron east of the Mermentau. Jim Bradshaw, *"C'est Vrai," The Daily Advertiser,* August 24, 2004, p. 2B.

76. Glenn R. Conrad, *Land Records of the Attakapas District,* Vol. 1, The Attakapas Doomsday Book: *Land Grants, Claims and Confirmations in the Attakapas District 1764-1826,* (University of Southwestern Louisiana, Lafayette, Louisiana, Center for Louisiana Studies, 1990).

77. Document recorded in Volume 1 (1760-1779) of the Clerk of Courts office of St. Martin Parish, Louisiana. Grover Rees translated the document. The Joseph Broussard listed in the document is not *Beausoleil* because he had died in 1765. Historical journalist Jim Bradshaw wrote: "The present church at St. Martinville bears an inscription saying that it was established in 1765. But this was probably the date that the congregation was formed, not when the first building went up. There may have been a small chapel of some sort at St. Martinville then, but the first real church apparently came nearly a decade later. Even after it was built, the St. Martinville church went for another decade before getting its first resident pastor. Priests from Pointe Coupée and Opelousas ministered in St. Martinville. Father George Murphy took charge of the church in 1791, and he is generally credited with being the first to refer to it as being dedicated to *St. Martin de Tours.* Before that, it was called *l'Elise de la Nouvelle-Acadie aux Attakapas,* the Church of New Acadia at Attakapas. Jim Bradshaw, *"C'est Vrai," The Daily Advertiser,* August 17, 2004, p. 4A.

78. Vermilion Historical Society, *History of Vermilion Parish, Louisiana,* 2 Vols. (Dallas: Taylor Publishing Company, 1983-2003).

79. General Curney J. Dronet, *A Century of Acadian Culture - The Development of a Cajun Community: Erath* (Acadian Heritage and Culture Foundation, Erath, Louisiana, 2000).

80. Chris Segura, "Broussard Family Group Gets Non-Profit Status," *The Sunday Advertiser,* December 14, 1996.

81. The author, in a letter dated May 29, 1997, proposed the memorial as well as an archaeological project to locate *Beausoleil's* gravesite.

82. James F. Broussard, *Pour Parler Francais* (D.C. Health and Co., Boston, 1921).

83. *Congrès Mondial Acadien Louisiane 1999,* "Broussard Family Has Rich History," *The Sunday Advertiser,* July 7, 1996, Section D.

84. Jacques M. Henry and Carl L. Bankston, II, *Blue Collar Bayou* (Praeger Press, Westport, Connecticut, 2002), p. 2. "In an effort to get the message across that there's more to Acadiana than *laissez les bons temps rouler,* a variety of activities are slated for the inaugural Acadian Heritage Week on Sept. 11-19 [2004]. Spearheaded by musician Zachary Richard and the Committee for Acadian Heritage Week — the plan is to develop a greater awareness of the history and culture of the Acadian people the week prior to and concluding with *Festivals Acadiens.* Another objective is the inclusion of a revised curriculum of Acadian history in the Louisiana history classes in the eighth grade statewide. 'The idea began in order to educate people a little bit more about our Acadian history,' said David Cheramie, executive director of the Council for the Development of French in Louisiana. Barry Jean Ancelet, professor of French and folklore at the University of Louisiana at Lafayette, said while Acadiana consists of many intertwined cultures that have 'made our culture what it is and enriches us from our tables to our dancehalls — I think there is room, at the same time, to focus on one of the most important influences on our culture and that is

the Acadian culture. I think that's a very important aspect of how we live here in south Louisiana. We need to know where we come from,' Ancelet said. Ancelet attended the *Congrès Mondial Acadien* in Nova Scotia in August and saw how Acadians from around the world gathered and discussed their common heritage. 'We are different in significant ways, and we can only figure out how that happened if we compare who we were, and who we might have been, with who we actually did become,' he said. Looking ahead to next year's event, Ancelet said 2005 is the 250th anniversary of the Acadian exile. 'Now one might wonder why would any people celebrate one of the worst catastrophes in its history,' said Ancelet. 'But there's a very simple reason: Because we're still here to celebrate. Because we are still here thriving. Because the intent of the exile, which was to eliminate Acadie, actually produced numerous Acadies. It proliferated us and I think we should make note of that. And what better place to do that than here in Louisiana, in perhaps the most significant result for the exile.' A resolution introduced by state Rep. Clara G. Baudoin in the Legislature has designated the third week of September as 'Acadian Heritage Week.' For information, call (337) 291-5474, or visit the Internet at http://www.acadianheritage. org." Dominick Cross, "Heritage Week to focus on contributions of Acadians," *The Advocate*, September 2, 2004, p. 9 B.

CHAPTER 11 - THE PETITION

85. Ibid., footnote 11, p. 216. James H. Schlarman, *From Quebec to New Orleans*, (Buechler Publishing company, Bellville, Illinois, 1929), p. 313. For a detailed discussion of these issues, please see the article, "The Petition to Obtain an Apology for the Acadian Deportation: Warren A. Perrin, et al versus Great Britain, et al," *Southern University Law Review*, Vol. 27, No. 1, Fall 1999.

86. The parish register of *Saint-Charles-aux-mines* church in Grand Pré was carried to Louisiana by the deportees, a unique witness to the journey of the prisoners who were held a month in the Grand Pré church awaiting the boats of the deportation. These records of births, baptisms and marriages cover the years 1707-1748 and are presently in the possession of the Catholic Diocese of Baton

Rouge, Department of the Archives, P. O. Box 2028, Baton Rouge, Louisiana, 70821-2028. *The Advocate,* August 9, 1998.

87. Ibid., p.63.

88. Ibid., footnote 39, p. 1: "Their judges were also their prosecutors." For a transcript of the judicial proceedings authorizing the dispersal see: Thomas B. Aikens, ed., *Acadian and Nova Scotia: Documents Relating to the Acadian French and the First British Colonization of the Province, 1714-1758,* 2nd edition (Cottonport, La., 1972), pp. 247-267. Condemning an entire population for the actions of a few is reminiscent [of the mass execution of civilians by German soldiers, a crime against humanity] of St. Ours, France, during World War II.

89. Jean Daigle, *The Acadians of the Maritime: Thematic Studies* (University of Moncton, Moncton, New Brunswick, 1982).

CHAPTER 12 – APOLOGIES

90. Joseph G. Tregle, Jr., "The History of Louisiana" (Louisiana State University Press, Baton Rouge, Louisiana, 1977), p. 125. Following the exile, Acadians were preoccupied with survival. Yet, it is surprising to note that their oral literature, which is so rich in other respects, contains very few traces of the deportation or years in exile. Those themes were first dealt with by foreign writers who created the literary myth of Acadia, paradise lost, of a martyred people who are resigned and faithful.

CHAPTER 13 - SUPPORT FOR THE PETITION

91. Ron Delhomme, "The Queen on Trial," *The Daily Advertiser,* August 13, 1999.

92. Griffin Smith, Jr., "The Cajuns - Still Loving Life," *National Geographic* magazine, Volume 178, No. 4, October, 1999, p. 57.

93. Eric Lawlor, "The One Man Acadian Liberation Front," *Los Angeles Times Magazine,* September 4, 1994, p. 26.

94. Louise McKinney, "Perrin's Petition," *The World and I,* September, 1995, pp. 206-215.

95. Jonathan Ledgard, "An Old British Crime: Cajuns' Belated Counterattack," *The Economist,* January 31-February 6, 1998, p. 32.

CHAPTER 14 - THE ROYAL PROCLAMATION

96. Marsha Sills, "Queen Elizabeth II offers apology for deporting Acadians," *The Advertiser,* December 11, 2003; Ron Thibodeaux "Royal regrets offered for Acadian expulsion," *The Times-Picayune,* December 11, 2003; Associated Press, "Canadian remorse on Acadians official," *The Advocate,* December 11, 2003; Associated Press, "Houma: Canadian apology is bittersweet," *The Advertiser,* December 12, 2003; Judy Stanford, "Journey's end," *The Sunday Advertiser,* August 1, 2004. "On August 9, 2004, the Grand-Pré Historic Site hosted several activities dedicated to Louisiana's Acadians including music, food and a presentation by the author. The day was titled 'Cajuns Come Home to Grand Pré.' Lafayette resident Warren Perrin will speak on a Royal Proclamation issued by Queen Elizabeth II, in which she apologized for the English expulsion of the Acadians from the Maritime Provinces beginning in 1755. Perrin will also sign copies of his book 'Acadian Redemption: From *Beausoleil* Broussard to the Queen's Royal Proclamation.'" Cheré Coen, "Congrès devotes day to Louisiana cousins, " *The Daily Advertiser,* August 9, 2004, p. 1A.

97. Eve Berger *"Echos':Torts Historiques," France -Louisiane,* Paris, France, No. 114, September - December, 2003.

98. Steve Hanchey, *"Warren Perrin ravi de la proclamation royale," L'Acadie NOUVELLE,* December 12, 2003; Canadian Press, "Suffering of Acadian deportation recognized in royal proclamation," *The Mail Star/The Chronicle-Herald,* December 11, 2003; Brian Underhill, "Comeau wants expulsion probe," *The Mail Star/The Chronicle-Herald,* December 4, 2003 and Susan Bradley, "Apology accepted," *The Chronicle-Herald,* July 31, 2004. "On one occasion, I was at a function in Britain and somehow found myself in the receiving line

for Prince Charles. A group of Palestinians ahead of me implored him to support their cause, so when the heir to the British throne fixed his gaze upon me, I brought up my own people's grievance. 'It's almost 250 years after the fact,' I informed the Prince, 'but Acadians are still looking to your mother to apologize for the expulsion of our ancestors.' Pausing ever so slightly, he replied with a hint of a royal wink: 'History can be so cruel.'" Lyse Doucet, "We're born again," *The Globe and Mail,* July 31, 2004, p. F4.

99. David Ljunggren, "Canada acknowledges wrong done to Acadians deported in 1700s," *The Boston Globe,* December 11, 2003; Beurmond Banville, "Acadians to get apology from Queen Elizabeth, "*The Bangor Daily News,* December 5, 2003; and Clifford Krauss, "Evangeline's people gather and weep for ancestors' fate," *New York Times,* August 12, 2004.

100. Irene B. Guidry, *In Written Word - The Cajun Way,* p. 30, a forthcoming book.

101. J. Maxie Broussard, "Minutes of Gathering," *Gazette Beausoleil,* Vol. VI, Spring, 2004, p. 2 and *France-Louisiane, "Le Grand Dérangement Reconnu!,"* No. 116, April-June, 2004, p. 8.

102. Louisiana Public Broadcasting, "Louisiana-The State We're In," aired June 16, 2004; Canadian Broadcasting Corporation, "Canadian Experience" Toronto, Canada, interview by Grazyna Krupa, "Expulsion," September 9, 2004; CBS affiliate KLFY, Lafayette, Louisiana, aired December 11, 2004 and ABC affiliate KATC, Lafayette, Louisiana, aired December 11, 2004; Linda Boudreaux, "The Extra Mile," Acadiana Open Channel TV, August 3, 2004; and John Darling Haynes, untitled documentary film on Acadian culture, to be aired in the fall of 2004, June 10, 2004.

103. Trent Angers, "Queen of England Apologizes for Acadian Expulsion," *Acadiana Profile,* Vol. 23 No. 4 February, 2004; Bucky McMahon, "Warren Perrin Defender Of The Cajuns," *Esquire,* June, 2004, p. 123; David Wallace McDonald, *National Geographic Magazine* interview June, 2004 and Jeffrey Houdlett, "The Cajun Connection,"

Portland Magazine, Vol. 19, No. 4, 2004, pp. 55-57.

104. Our Views, "Today's Apology for distant evils," *The Advocate*, December 26, 2003; Another Voice, "Righting a Wrong," *The Times*, February 4, 2004, p. 19; "Atoning for Acadia" *Times-Picayune*, December 15, 2003; "Good: All Apologies" *Times of Acadiana*, December 17, 2003, Vol. 24, No. 13 and Comment, "Acadians Mark 400," *Capte Breton Post*, August 14, 2004, p. A8.

105. Carl A. Brasseaux, *In Search of Evangeline: Origins and Evolution of the Evangeline Myth* (Blue Heron Press, Thibodaux, Louisiana, 1989).

106. Ibid., footnote 25, 3:166.

107. Carl A. Brasseaux, *Acadian to Cajun: Transformation of a People, 1803-1877* (University Press of Mississippi, Jackson, Mississippi, 1992).

108. Alexandra Zavis, Associated Press, "Ethnic slaughter prompts refugee crisis in Sudan," *Sunday Advocate*, July 11, 2004, p. 18A.

109. Henry Wadsworth Longfellow, *Evangeline: A Tale of Acadie*, in *The Political Works of Henry Wadsworth Longfellow* (Houghton Mifflin, New York, 1886), 2: pp. 19-106. Vaughn Madden, *Congrès* general manager, said the two-week event surpassed expectations, especially on the emotional front. The links made between Acadians and Cajuns, she said, overwhelmed feelings at times. "It was about creating ties around the world." Madden said Nova Scotia residents proved hospitable to the visitors from far away. "They opened their homes and shared stories." One story she heard was about a property owner who, when approached at 10 p.m., allowed a family from Louisiana to camp overnight on their ancestral lands. Others allowed practical strangers to pitch tents in back yards. According to Madden, the number of visitors was close to the anticipated 250,000. "For example, Clare district usually gets 5,000 tourists a season," Madden said. "They had over 25,000 this year already." Wendy Elliot, "A chance to celebrate," *The Daily Advertiser*, August 22, 2004, p. 1G. "This year, however, attending the 2004 *Congrès* for Cajuns was more than family reunions, ceremonies and festivals in

Nova Scotia. It was a chance to come home. It was a time to stand with cousins from all over the world on the land their ancestors settled. It was a chance to gaze over the rivers, valleys and enormous tides that a united people once viewed as they reclaimed land from the sea while settling l'Acadie, before the wars would decimate their lives and the English would force them from their homes beginning in 1755. Two hundred and fifty years since *le Grand Dérangement* but the lure of the ancestral land still beckoned." Cheré Coen, "A chance to come home," *The Daily Advertiser*, August 22, 2004, p. 1G. The Prime Minister of Canada Paul Martin, Nova Scotian Premier John Hamm, Lt. Governor Myra Freeman and Louisiana Governor Kathleen Babineaux Blanco participated in the Congrès' closing mass and ceremonies on August 15, 2004. At the beginning of the French mass, water brought from the MiKmaq people and from France, Belgium, Acadie, Quebec, Louisiana and New England was poured into a container as a sign of reconciliation. Governor Kathleen Babineaux Blanco celebrated Acadian heritage worldwide as she spoke before thousands assembled at the closing ceremonies of *Congrès Mondial Acadien* in Grand Pré, Nova Scotia. "This land, the one that our ancestors settled, is our ancestral home and one that we love," Blanco said. "All Acadians, wherever they live," Blanco said, "can feel pride in having transformed not only expulsion, but also modern day discrimination and exclusion into global success." The crowd, 10,000 strong, gave Blanco's emotional speech a standing ovation. Later, Blanco spoke about a renewed interest in French immersion programs in Louisiana schools. "Even adults," she noted, "gather in places such as Lafayette for breakfast sessions to practice their French." Wendy Elliott, "Blanco thankful for ancestral pilgrimage during this year's *Congrès*." *The Daily Advertiser*, August 18, 2004, p. 1D.

In 2002, Warren A. Perrin was photographed holding the Acadian flag in front of the Acadian Museum of Erath.

Photo by Kermit Boullion.

ABOUT THE AUTHOR

Warren A. Perrin was born March 11, 1947, in the hamlet of Henry, located in Vermilion Parish, Louisiana. He graduated from Henry High School in 1965, the University of Louisiana at Lafayette in 1969, and Louisiana State University Law School in 1972. In 1969, he married Mary Leonise Broussard. After law clerking for Judge J. Cleveland Frugé at the Third Circuit Court of Appeal, Perrin founded the firm of Perrin, Landry, deLaunay, Dartez and Ouellet with offices in Lafayette, Erath, Broussard and Maurice.

In 1990, Perrin and his good friend, J. Weldon Granger, established the non-profit Acadian Heritage and Culture Foundation, Inc., which operates the Acadian Museum of Erath. The museum is supported by many volunteers from Erath. Financial support is provided by donations and sales of the book *A Century of Acadian Culture*. In 1996, the Acadian Museum established the "Order of Living Legends," which, under the directorship of Kermit Bouillion, honors individuals who helped shape and promote the French culture of Louisiana.

For fifteen years, Perrin spearheaded a campaign to compel Queen Elizabeth II of England to acknowledge and apologize for the Acadians' expulsion from Nova Scotia. In January 1990, with the support and urging of many, Perrin presented a Petition on behalf of the Acadian people to the British government and Crown seeking an apology for the deportation of the Acadians from Nova Scotia in 1755. In recognition of this accomplishment, the French-American Chamber of Commerce honored him on January 20, 2004, with a special Cultural Achievement award. On August 11, 2004, the Broussard Family organization of Louisiana, *La Famille Beausoleil*, recognized Perrin for his achievements.

In 1993, Perrin represented the United States at the World Human Rights Conference held in Normandy, France, where he made a presentation on his Petition for an apology. Subsequently, he founded the Human Rights Conference held in conjunction with *Festival International de Louisiane*, which annually presented programs dealing with cultural and minority rights.

In 1994, Governor Edwin Edwards named Perrin to serve as President of the Council for the Development of French in Louisiana, or CODOFIL. He was reappointed in 1996 by Governor Foster and in 2004 by Governor Blanco. Perrin has worked tirelessly to promote the

Francophone culture. He has developed new initiatives, programs and organizations to involve the African-Americans and Creoles, and the Houma Indian people of Louisiana in the movement to restore pride in their unique cultures. In recognition, he was the recipient of the "Cajun of the Year" award by the Cajun French Music Association.

In recognition of his leadership role in the Acadian community of North America, Perrin was invited to be a featured speaker at the 1994 World Acadian Reunion in Moncton, New Brunswick. Following that event, he was instrumental in having Louisiana host the Second World Acadian Reunion in Louisiana in 1999 as part of *FrancoFête '99*, an idea he promoted to help celebrate the state's tricentennial in 1999. In support of that initiative, Perrin served as President of a task force appointed by then-Lieutenant Governor Kathleen Babineaux Blanco, to carry out this year-long event comprising of over 1,500 separate cultural celebrations.

Since 1979, Perrin has been an adjunct professor at the University of Louisiana at Lafayette. Further, he was the co-founder of the Francophone Section of the Louisiana Bar Association and the Babineaux International Civil Law Symposium. In recognition of those efforts, he was given the award of *L'Ecole de Droit* by the University of Moncton in 1991.

From 1993-94 Perrin served as President of the University of Louisiana at Lafayette Alumni Association. In 1987, he was inducted into UL of Lafayette's Athletic Hall of Fame for his athletic achievements: he was a member of the then-University of Southwestern Louisiana Weightlifting Teams that won the National Collegiate Weightlifting Championships in 1966, 1967 and 1968.

In May, 2000, his family honored his father's memory by establishing the Henry L. Perrin Memorial Endowed Scholarship at University of Louisiana at Lafayette, which annually awards a scholarship to two Vermilion Parish High School graduates. Additionally, in 2001, Perrin's law firm established the Memorial Endowed Scholarship for French Immersion studies at University of Louisiana at Lafayette which provides funds to send students to attend *Sainte-Anne Université* in Nova Scotia.

He serves on the Board of Directors of Friends of French Studies at LSU, and has been a panelist for legal seminars at LSU Law Center.

Perrin has been the subject of many interviews which have been broadcast nationally and internationally, including *National Public Radio, TV 5 North American, USA National TV Network, the BBC of London,* the CBC of Canada and CBS's morning news show *Sunday Morning.*

Perrin has been honored with the following awards:

1997   Representative of the State of Louisiana at the World Francophone Summit, Hanoi, Vietnam;

1998   Cajun French Music Association's "Heritage Award;"

1999   "Outstanding Businessman of Acadiana," *The Times of Acadiana*;

1999   Honorary "Doctorate of Laws," degree *Université Sainte-Anne*, Nova Scotia and "French National Order of Merit" conferred by President Jacques Chirac of France;

2000   "Distinguished Service Award," Louisiana Restaurant Association and "Louisiana Rural Tourism Success Award," LSU Louisiana Sea Grant Program;

2001   "International Achievement Award," International Trade Development Group;

2002   "Order of Merit," The Council for French and Cultural Development, Quebec, Canada;

2003   "Cultural Preservation Award" by Vermilionville;

2004a "Cultural Achievement Award" by the French-American Chamber of Commerce

2004b "Beausoleil Award" by *La Famille Beausoleil* during the Broussard Family Reunion on August 11, 2004; and the

2004c "Pioneer Award" by the Abbeville Cultural and Historical Alliance.

In 1999, Perrin was named by Speaker of the Louisiana House of Representatives Charles Dewitt to serve on the Louisiana Purchase Bicentennial Commission which organized that year-long celebration and served as Chairman of the International Relations Committee. In 2003, Perrin was named as a Honorary Chevalier by the Giant Omelette Festival of Abbeville, and "Goodwill Ambassador" by the City of Lafayette. Perrin's work in promoting the French culture has elevated him to the forefront of leading cultural activists, and has helped to reinvigorate the Cajun pride movement through his Petition for an apology, the establishment of the Acadian Museum and his many ongoing CODOFIL activities.

General Curney J. Dronet, Sr.

BIBLIOGRAPHY

Akins, Thomas B., *Acadian and Nova Scotia: Documents Relating to the Acadian French and the First British Colonization of the Province, 1714-1758*, 2nd edition (Cottonport, Louisiana, 1972).

Akins, *Selections for the Public Documents of the Province of Nova Scotia* (Annand, 1869).

Ancelet, Dr. Barry and Morgan, Elmore, Jr., *The Makers of Cajun Music* (University of Texas Press, 1984).

Ancelet, Dr. Barry Jean, Edwards, Jay and Pitre, Glen *Cajun Country* (University Press of Mississippi, 1991).

Angers, Trent, publisher, "Queen of England Apologizes for Acadian Expulsion," *Acadiana Profile*, Vol. 23, No. 4, February, 2004.

Arsenault, Bona, *History of the Acadians* (Ottawa, 1988).

Arsenault, Georges, *The Island Acadians 1720-1980* (Ragweek Press Charlottetown, 1989).

Associated Press, "Canadian remorse on Acadians official", *The Advocate*, December 11, 2003.

Associated Press, "Houma: Canadian apology is bittersweet", *The Advertiser*, December 12, 2003.

Babineau, René, *Brief History of Acadia 1604-1988* (Copyright Printing, Inc., 1988).

Banville, Beurmond, "Acadians to get apology from Queen Elizabeth", *The Bangor Daily News*, December 5, 2003.

Basque, Maurice, "*Conflits Et Solidarités Familiales Dams: Ancienne Acadie: L'Affaire Broussard De 1724*", La Société Historique Acadienne, Les Cahiers, Vol. 20, No. 2, *Avril-Juin* 1989.

Basque, Maurice "*Genre et gestion du pouvoir communautaire à Annapolis Royal au 18e siècle,*" *Dalhousie Law Journal*, Vo. 17, No. 2, Fall 1994.

Bernard, Antoine, *Le Drame Acadien* (Montreal, 1925).

Bernard, Dr. Shane K., *The Cajuns - Americanization of a People* (University Press of Mississippi, Jackson, Mississippi, 2003).

Bliss Carman, *the Vengeance of Noel Broussard - A Tale of the Acadian Expulsion* (The University Press of Cambridge, Massachusetts, 1919, p. 13).

Bradley, Susan, "Apology accepted," *The Chronicle Herald*, July 31, 2004.

Bradshaw, Jim, "Broussard Led Acadians to Attakapas Area," *The Daily Advertiser*, Supplement: History of Acadiana, March 20, 1999.

Bradshaw, Jim, "*C'est Vrai,*" *The Daily Advertiser*, August 17, 2004.

Bradshaw, Jim, "UL Lafayette Acquires 1755 Letter," *The Daily Advertiser,* October 20, 2001.

Brasseaux, Dr. Carl A., *Scattered To The Wind: Dispersal And Wanderings Of The Acadians, 1755-1809* (USL Center for Louisiana Studies, 1991).

Brasseaux, Dr. Carl A., *Quest for the Promised Land* (USL Center for Louisiana Studies, 1989).

Brasseaux, Dr. Carl A., *In Search of Evangeline: Origins and Evolution of the Evangeline Myth* (Thibodeaux, Louisiana, 1989).

Brasseaux, Dr. Carl A., *Acadian to Cajun: Transformation of a People, 1803-1877* (University Press of Mississippi, 1992).

Brasseaux, Dr. Carl A., *The Founding of New Acadia: The Beginnings of Acadian Life In Louisiana, 1765-1803* (Louisiana State University Press, 1987).

Brasseaux, Dr. Carl A, *Lafayette* (Windsor Publications, Inc., 1990).

Brebner, J. B., *New England Outpost: Acadia Before The Conquest Of Canada* (New York, 1927).

Brebner, John Bartlet, *New England's Outpost* (Columbia University Press, New York, 1927).

Brenner, John B., "Canadian Policy Towards the Acadians in 1751," *Canadian Historical Review,* Vol. 12, No. 3, 1931.

Brochure, *Fort Beauséjour National Historical Site* (Parks Canada, 1966).

Broussard, Alton E., "Were Early Acadian Men Really the Docile Type?," *The Daily Advertiser,* November, 1977.

Broussard, Emery J. and Lorraine Broussard Campbell, *Vermilion Historical Society, History of Vermilion Parish, Vol. II* (Taylor Publishing Co., Dallas, Texas).

Broussard, J. Maxie, "Minutes of Gathering," *Gazette Beausoleil,* Vol. VI, Spring, 2004.

Broussard, Dr. James F., *Pour Parler Francais* (D.C. Health and Col, Boston, Massachusetts, 1921).

Brun, R., "Amherst Papers," *la Societé Historique Acadienne* (Moncton, New Brunswick, 1970).

Calhoun, Milburn, *Louisiana Almanac* 1995-96 (Pelican Publishing, 1995).

Carman, Bliss, *The Vengeance of Noel Broussad - A Tale of the Acadian Expulsion* (The University Press of Cambridge, Massachusetts, 1919).

Canadian Press, "Suffering of Acadian deportation recognized in royal proclamation," *The Mail Star/The Chronicle-Herald,* December 11,

2003.

Chaisson, Father Anselme, *Chéticamp: History and Acadian Traditions* (Breakwater Books Ltd., 1986).

Chandler, R. E., "End Of An Odyssey: Acadians Arrive In St. Gabriel, Louisiana," *Louisiana History XIV* (1974).

Chevrier, Cécile, *Acadie: Sketches of a Journey* (La Société Nationale de l'Acadie, 1994).

Clark, Andrew Hill, *Acadia: The Geography of Early Nova Scotia to 1760* (The University of Wisconsin Press, 1968).

Clark, George Frederick, *Expulsion of the Acadians* (Brunswick Press, 1955).

Coen, Cheré, "Congrès devotes day to Louisiana cousins," *The Daily Advertiser*, August 9, 2004.

Comeaux, Malcolm L., *Atchafalaya Swamp Life - Settlement and Folk Occupations*, (Louisiana State University Press, Baton Rouge, 1972).

Comment, "Acadians Mark 400," *Capte Breton Post*, August 14, 2004.

Condow, James E., *The Deportation of the Acadians* (Parks Canada, 1986).

Conrad, Glenn R., *The Cajuns: Essays on their History and Culture*, (USL Center for Louisiana Studies, Lafayette, Louisiana, 1978).

Conrad, Glenn R., *Land Records of the Attakapas District*, Volume 1, *The Attakapas Domesday Book: Land Grants,Claims and Confirmations in the Attakapas District 1764-1826*. (USL Center for Louisiana Studies, Lafayette, Louisiana, 1990).

Conrad, Glenn R., *Dictionary of Louisiana Biography*, "Joseph *dit Beausoleil* Broussard," (Louisiana Historical Association and Center for Louisiana Studies, University of Southwestern Louisiana, Lafayette, Louisiana, 1988).

Congrès Mondial Acadien Louisiane 1999, "Broussard Family Has Rich History," *Sunday Advertiser*, July 7, 1996, Section D.

Cormier, Clément, *"Jean-Francois Brossard (Broussard)"*, *Dictionnaire Biographique du Canada*, Vol. III (10 vols.; Quebec, Canada, 1974).

Cougle, R. James, *Not By Choice: The True Story of the French-English Struggle* (Fredericton, 1992).

Cross, Dominique, "Heritage Week to focus on contributions of Acadians," *The Advocate*, September 2, 2004.

Daigle, Pierre, *Tears, Love and Laughter: The Story Of The Cajuns* (Swallow Publications, Inc., 1987).

Daigle, Jean, *The Acadians of the Maritimes: Thematic Studies* (University of Moncton, 1982).

Daigle, Rev. Msgr. Jules O., *A Dictionary of the Cajun Language* (Edwards Bros., Inc. 1984).

Dainow, Joseph, *Civil Code of Louisiana* (West Publishing Co., 1961).

Davis, Stephen A., *Micmac* (Four East Publications, 1990).

DeCard, Frank, *Louisiana Sojourns* (L.S.U. Press, 1998).

Deveau, J. Alphonse, *Two Beginnings: A Brief Acadian History* (Lescarbot Publications, 1992).

Deveau, J. Alphonse, *Le Chef des Acadiens (Les Editions Lescarbot,* Yarmoth, Nova Scotia, 1980), 2nd Edition.

Domengeaux, James H., "Native-Born Acadians And The Equality Ideal," *Louisiana Law Review,* Vol. 46, No. 6, July, 1986.

Doiron, Jeannot, *Le pays de "la Cadie"* (by author, Canada, 2004).

Doucet, Lyse, "We're born again," *The Globe and Mail,* July 31, 2004.

Doucette, Michel, *Le Congrès Mondial Acadien (Les Editions d'Acadie,* 1996).

Doughty, Arthur G., *The Acadian Exiles* (Toronto, Canada, 1920).

Dronet, General Curney J., *A Century of Acadian Culture - The Development of a Cajun Community: Erath* (Acadian Heritage and Culture Foundation, Inc., Erath, Louisiana, 2000).

Dupon, Albert Leonce, "The Career of Paul Octave Hebert, Governor of Louisiana 1853-1856," *Louisiana Historical Quarterly,* XXXI."

d'Entremont, *"The Baronnie de Pombcoup and the Acadians,"* The Yarmouth *Herald-Telegram,* 1931.

d'Entremont *"Historie de Pubnico"* in *Les régions acadiennes de la Nouvelle-Écosse, (Centre Acadien, Université Sainte-Anne,* 1982).

d'Entremont, C.J., *"Joseph Brossard (Broussard) dit Beausoleil," Dictionnaire Biographique du Canada,* Vol. III, De 1741 á 1770 (Toronto, Canada, 1974).

Editorial, "Atoning for Acadia", *The Times-Picayne,* December 15, 2003.

Editorial, "Our Views, today's apology for distant evils," *The Advocate,* December 26, 2003.

Editorial, "Another Voice, Righting a Wrong", *The Times,* February 4, 2004.

Elliott, Wendy, "Blanco thankful for ancestral pilgrimage during this year's Congrès," *The Daily Advertiser,* August 18, 2004.

Faragher, Dr. John Mack, *A Great and Noble Scheme: The Expulsion of the*

French Acadians (New York: W.W. Norton, 2005).

Faragher, Dr. John Mack, private email to author, September 7, 2004.

Fuller, Reese R., "Living Ind Finds," *The Independent*, August 25, 2004.

Gendron, Gilbert, "The British Genocide of the Acadian People," *The Barnes Review*, Vol. III, No. 10, October, 1997.

Giraud, Marcel, *A History of French Louisiana* (Louisiana State University Press, 1958).

Griffin, Harry Lewis, *A Brief History of the Acadians*, from an address delivered at a meeting of *France-Amerique de la Louisiane Acadienne* at the College of Sacred Heart, Grand Coteau, Louisiana, October 18, 1952.

Griffiths, Naomi E.S., *The Acadians of the British Sea-Port*, "Acadiensis 4" (1976).

Griffiths, Naomi E. S., *The Acadians: Creation of a People* (McGraw-Hill Ryerson Ltd., 1973).

Griffiths, Naomi E. S., *The Contexts of Acadian History, 1686-1784* (McGill-Queen's University Press, 1976).

Griffiths, Naomi E. S., *The Contexts of Acadian History 1686-1784* (Toronto, 1992).

Guidry, Irene B., *In Written Words - The Cajun Way*, a forthcoming book.

Guirard, Leona Martin, *St. Martinville - The Land of Evangeline in Picture Story* (self-published, 1950).

Haliburton, Thomas C., *An Historical and Statistical Account of Nova Scotia* (J. Howe, 1829).

Hanchey, Steve, "*Warren Perrin ravi de la proclamation royale*," *L'Acadie NOUVELLE*, December 12, 2003.

Hannay, James, *The History of Acadia* (J. & J. McMillan, 1879).

Hebert, Rev. Donald J., *Southwest Louisiana Records*, (Hebert Publications, Louisiana), Volume 1A.

Henry, Jacques, "From Acadien to Cajun to Cadien: Ethnic Labelization and Construction of Identity," *Journal of American Ethnic History*, Vol. 17 No. 4, Summer, 1998.

Henry, Jacques M. and Carl L. Bankston, II, *Blue Collar Bayou* (Praeger Press, Westport, Connecticut, 2002).

Herbin, John Frederic, *The History of Grand-Pré* (Heritary Books, Inc., 1891).

Hirsch, Arnold R. and Logsdon, Joseph *Creole New Orleans - Race and Americanization* (LSU Press, 1992).

Hoffman, Paul E., editor, *The Louisiana Purchase and Its People* (Louisiana Historical Association and the Center for Louisiana Studies, UL at

Lafayette, 2004).

Houdlett, Jeffery, "The Cajun Connection," *Portland Magazine*, Vol. 19, No. 4, 2004.

Ignatieff, Michael, "Truth, Justice and Reconciliation," *National Canadian Bar Association*, Vol. 5, No. 7, November/December, 1997.

Jekel, Pamela, *Bayou* (Kensington Publishing Co., 1991).

Jen, Janet, *Acadiana Genealogy Exchange*, Vol. XXVI, April/July, 1997.

Kennedy, W.P.M., *The Commission of Canada 1534-1937* (Russell & Russell, New York, 1973).

Krauss, Clifford, "Evangeline's people gather and weep for ancestors' fate," *New York Times*, August 12, 2003.

Lauriere, Emile, *La Tragedie d'un Peuple* (Paris, 1922), Vol. I.

LeBlanc, Dudley J., *The Acadian Miracle* (Evangeline Publishing Company, 1966).

LeBlanc, Dudley J., *The True Story of the Acadians* (by author, Lafayette, Louisiana, 1937).

LeBlanc, Robert G., "The Acadian Migration," *Canadian Geographical Journal*, 81 (1970).

LeBlanc, Ronnie Gilles, *Joseph Broussard dit Beausoleil (Cahiers de la Societé historique Acadienne* 52, 1986), Vol. 17, No. 2.

Ledgard, Jonathan, "An Old British Crime: Cajuns' Belated Counter-Attack," *The Economist*, January 31, 1998.

Leger, Senator Viola, *News From the Senate*, Vol. 1, No. 3, June, 2004.

Ljunggren, David, "Canada acknowledges wrong done to Acadians deported in 1700s", *The Boston Globe*, December 11, 2003.

Longfellow, Henry Wadsworth, *Evangeline: A Tale of Acadie, The Political Words of Henry Wadsworth Longfellow* (Houghton Mifflin, New York, 1886).

Louisiana Public Broadcasting, "Louisiana - The State We're In," May 16, 2004.

MacGregor, Dawson, R., *The Government of Canada*, 4th ed., (University of Toronto Press, 1966).

Mahaffie, Charles D., Jr., *A Land of Discord Always: Acadia From its Beginnings to the Expulsion of Its People, 1604-1755* (Down East Books, 1995).

Maillet, Antoinine, *Pélagie*, translated by Phillip Stafford (New Press, 1970).

Marcantel, David, "The Legal Status of French in Louisiana", *Revue des Parlementaires de Langue Française*, Fall, 1994.

Marshall, Dianne, *Georges Island - The Keep of Halifax Harbour* (Nimbus

Publishing, Halifax, Nova Scotia, 2003).

McCreath, Peter L. and Leefe, John G., *A History of Early Nova Scotia* (Four East Publications, 1982).

Melancon, Brenda, *The History of Sorrento* (Franklin Press, Inc., 1996).

Murdoch, Beamish, *History of Nova Scotia* (James Barnes, 1865).

Paradis, Roger, *Papers of Prudent L. Mercure Histoire du Madawaska* (Madawaska Historical Society, Maine, 1998).

Paratte, Henri-Dominique, *Peoples of the Maritimes - Acadians* (Nimbus Publishing, Toronto, California, 1998).

Paul, Daniel N., *The Confrontation of Micmac and European Civilizations* (Truro, Nova Scotia, Canada, 1993).

Paul, Daniel N., *We Were not Savages: A Micmac Perspective on the Collision of European and Aboriginal Civilization* (Nimbus Publishing Ltd., Halifax, Nova Scotia, 1993).

Paul, Daniel N., "MiKmaq, Acadians: friends then and now," *The Halifax Herald,* June 9, 2004.

Perrin, William Henry, *Southwest Louisiana Biographical and Historical* (The Gulf Publishing Co., 1891, reprinted by Claitor's Publishing Division, Baton Rouge, Louisiana, 1971).

Plank, Geoffrey, *An Unsettled Conquest* (University of Pennsylvania Press, Philadelphia, Pennsylvania, 2001).

Poesch, Jessie and Bacot, Barbara SoRelle, *Louisiana Buildings 1720-1994* (LSU Press, 1997).

Poirier, Leonie Comeau, *My Acadian Heritage* (Lancelot Press, 1989).

Quinpool, John, *First Things in Acadia* (First Things Publishers Ltd., 1936).

Reaux, Vita B. and John R., "Jean Francois Broussard and Catherine Richard," *Attakapas Gazette,* 6 (March, 1971).

Rees, Grover, translation, "The Dauterive Compact: Foundation of the Cattle Industry," *Attakapas Gazette,* 11 (Summer, 1976).

Richard, Edouard, *Acadia: Missing Links of a Chapter in American History* (Montreal, Canada, 1895).

Ricker, Darlene A., *L'sitkuk - The Story of the Bear River Mi'Kmaq Community,* (Roseway Publishing, Lockeport, Nova Scotia, 1997).

Ross, Sally and Deveau, Alphonse, *The Acadians of Nova Scotia: Past And Present* (Nimbus Publishing, 1992).

Rushton, William F., *The Cajuns* (New York, 1979).

Savary, A. W., *Supplement to the History of the County of Annapolis* (William

Briggs, 1913).

Savoy, Ann Allen, *Cajun Music: A Reflection Of A People* (Bluebird Press, 1984).

Schlarman, James H., *From Quebec to New Orleans*, (Buechler Publishing Company, Bellville, Illinois, 1929).

Ségalen, Jean, *Acadie en résistance* (Skal Vreigh-Montroules/Morlaix, France, 2002).

Segura, Chris, "La Famille Beausoleil Reunion Planned in Concert With Acadians Congrès," *The Daily Advertiser,* December 10, 1996.

Segura, Chris, "Broussard Family Group Gets Non-Profit Status," *The Sunday Advertiser,* December 14, 1996.

Silver, Alfred, private letter to author, August 21, 2004.

Silver, Alfred, *Three Hills Home* (Nimbus Publishing Ltd., Halifax, Nova Scotia, 2001).

Sills, Marsha, "Queen Elizabeth II offers apology for Deporting Acadians," *The Advertiser,* December, 11, 2003.

Simmoneaux, Angela, "All in the Family,*" The Sunday Advocate*, February 28, 1999.

Smith, Jr., Griffin, "The Cajuns - Still Loving Life," *National Geographic Magazine*, Vol. 178, No. 4, October, 1999.

Smith, Phillip H., *Acadia, A Lost Chapter In American History* (New York 1884).

St. Martin de Tours Catholic Church, *Copie d'un vieux registre* Archives, St. Martinville, Louisiana.

Stanford, Judy, "Journey's end," *The Daily Advertiser,* August 1, 2004.

Surette, Paul, *Petcoudiac: Colonisation et Destruction 1731-1755 (Les Editions d'Acadie,* 1988).

Surette, Paul, *La prée de l'Île et le Village-des-Beausoleil,* in Atlas *de L'Etablissement des Acadiens aux Trois Rivieres du Chignectou,* 1660-785 (*Editions d'Acadie,* 1996).

Surette, Roland F., *Métis/Acadian Heritage* 1604-2004 (Sentinel Printing Limited, Yarmouth, Nova Scotia, 2004).

Thibodeaux, Ron, "Acadian Homecoming," *The Times-Picayune*, August 22, 2004.

Thibodeaux, Ron, "Royal Regrets offered for Acadian expulsion," *The Times-Picayune,* December 11, 2003.

Tregle, Joseph G., Jr., *The History of Louisiana* (LSU Press, 1977).

Trenholm, Gladys, *A History of Fort Lawrence* (Sherwood Printing Ltd. 1985).

Trisch, Joseph Le Sage, *French in Louisiana* (A.F. Laborde and Sons, New

Orleans, 1959).

Underhill, Brian, "Comeau wants expulsion probe," *The Mail Star/The Chronicle-Herald,* December 4, 2003.

Vermilion Historical Society, *History of Vermilion Parish, Vol. I* (Taylor Publishing Company, 1983).

Vermilion Historical Society, *History of Vermilion Parish, Vol. II* (Taylor Publishing Company, 2003).

Vulliamy, Ed, "Fire in the Blood on the Bayou," *London Guardian Observer,* February 13, 1998.

Ward, Roger K., "The French Language in Louisiana Law and Legal Education: A Requiem" *Louisiana Law Review,* Vol. 57, No. 4, 1283, Summer, 1997.

Webster, J.C., *The Life of Thomas Pinchon.*

Webster, John Chance, *Acadia At The End Of The 17th Century* (Tribune Press, 1934).

West, Robert, *An Atlas of Louisiana Surnames of French and Spanish Origin* (Geoscience Publications, L.S.U.).

White, Stephen, lecture to the Broussard Family Reunion, Pomquet, Nova Scotia, August 13, 2004.

Wilson, Charles Regan and Ferris, William, *Encyclopedia Of Southern Culture* (University of North Carolina Press, 1989).

Winzerling, Rev. Oscar W., *Acadian Odyssey* (Louisiana State University Press, 1955).

Winslow, John, "Winslow's Journals," *Collections of the Nova Scotia Historical Society,* Boston, Massachusetts .

Zavis, Alexandra, Associated Press, "Ethnic slaughter prompts refugee crisis in Sudan," *Sunday Advocate,* July 11, 2004.

ORDER FORM

Order additional copies of Acadian Redemption: From *Beausoleil* Broussard to the Queen's Royal Proclamation by filling out and returning the form below.

I would like ___ copies of *Acadian Redemption: From* Beausoleil *Broussard to the Queen's Royal Proclamation* at $18.⁰⁰ each plus $4.⁰⁰ shipping and handling per book (Louisiana residents please add 9.75% sales tax - $1.⁷⁵). Please allow 15 days for delivery.

My check or money order for $_____.___ is enclosed.

Please charge my credit card:
❏MasterCard   ❏VISA   ❏American Express

*Card #*_____ *Exp. Date* _____

Signature _____

Name: _____

Address: _____

City/State/Zip: _____

Phone: _____ Email: _____

Please make your check payable and return to:
        Andrepont Publishing, L.L.C.
        326 Cedar Grove Drive
        Opelousas, LA 70570

Or order by:
        Phone: (Toll Free) 1-800-738-2500
        Fax: (337) 948-3492
        Email: publishing@andrepontprinting.com